The Fat Paddler

For Rebecca, Grace and Ella

The Fat Paddler

Sean Smith

FINCH PUBLISHING
SYDNEY

The Fat Paddler

First published in 2011 in Australia and New Zealand by Finch Publishing Pty Limited, ABN 49 057 285 248, Suite 2207, 4 Daydream Street, Warriewood, NSW, 2102, Australia.

13 12 11   8 7 6 5 4 3 2 1

The National Library of Australia Cataloguing-in-Publication entry:

Smith, Sean, 1972-.
The fat paddler / Sean Smith.
9781921462313 (pbk.)
Ex-football players–Rehabilitation.
Rugby football injuries.
Sports physical therapy.
Kayaking.

796.333

Edited by Pamela Hewitt
Editorial assistance by Megan Drinan
Text typeset in Chaparral by Pier Vido Design
Cover design by Peter Long
Cover image courtesy of Sean Smith
Printed by McPhersons Printing

All photos appearing in this book are courtesy of Sean Smith.

Finch titles can be viewed and purchased at **www.finch.com.au**

Contents

Foreword

I'T'S EASY TO READ THE TALES OF SPORTING GODS AND goddesses performing feats of superhuman endurance or strength, but it's equally easy to disassociate yourself from these tales. What we really want in a book is something we can relate to. We want to hear the tales of ordinary blokes, like ourselves, who battle with their weight, who struggle with their work–life balance, who enjoy maybe a drink too many on occasion but have the spirit not to accept that the terms have to be dictated to them.

In *The Fat Paddler*, Sean Smith takes us on an intensely personal journey of an ordinary bloke who has more than his fair share of faults. He was morbidly obese, grossly unfit, smoking and drinking too much. He was suffering from multiple health problems which were sustained from two life-threatening accidents and being caught up in the Bali bombing. (Luckily he was a rugby front rower, so some of his sins will be forgiven.)

The Fat Paddler represents all the values that we respect and admire in an Aussie bloke. He gets out there and gives it a go. For Sean, life hasn't been all estuary paddling, and it's the way he's fought through life's events that makes his story all the more motivating.

We strongly believe that 'adventure is relative'. No one can dictate or impose their notions of adventure upon you. Adventure is relative to all those experiences that have lead you to a certain point in your life: it's relative to your risk profile; it's relative to how you lead your life; it's relative only to you. The Fat Paddler has found a sport where he can constantly challenge himself and inspire others.

In late 2007 we went on our own little adventure. Over 62 days we paddled across one of the world's most treacherous stretches of ocean from Australia to New Zealand. We faced 10-metre towering waves, violent storms, terrifyingly close shark encounters and 14 days trapped in a current whirlpool. Finally, after 3318 kilometres and 1.7 million paddle strokes we finally staggered up the sands of New Zealand, underweight, bearded (well one of us!) and severely sleep deprived – but having learnt so much about ourselves and why adventure and living life to the fullest is so important. In reality, you don't have to paddle across an ocean or do something equally hare-brained to learn that life is not something to be squandered away in a job you hate, in a bar at 3 a.m. in the morning or in a bad relationship.

When we set off across the ditch, we had three goals: to have a helluva adventure; to be able to take the average person along for the ride with us; and maybe even to inspire one or two people to jump off their couches, away from their computers or TVs and head out on their own adventure. I'm glad that our story and journey has had an impact on Sean and the way that he views the challenges in his life, but to be completely honest the ethos and way that he lives his life is more humbling to us. This book, the FatPaddler.com website, the events and fundraising that Sean does cause waves that far outstrip the ripples of motivation spread by our journey.

Sean is out there in the paddling community extending his hand to the physically challenged (or as Sean puts it, the old, fat, injured, disabled or just plain lazy!) who want to take that first step of jumping off the couch but don't know how, or are daunted by the task.

Sean ... thanks for sharing mate, and we can't wait to see you on the water.

Cas and Jonesy (authors of *Crossing the Ditch*)
Two Fat paddlers in our own little way ...
March 2011

Prologue
Alone in the darkness

PUSHING OFF INTO THE INKY DARKNESS, I REPEATED my earlier check on equipment. Water supply replenished, food and energy gels restocked, GPS batteries still strong, maps turned to the right pages and warm paddle clothing all secured. It was 3 a.m., and the combination of sleep deprivation and physical exhaustion would soon make thinking through complex tasks impossible. I'd paddled 60 km down the mighty Hawkesbury River, but still had a gruelling 50 km to go.

Not that I wasn't already in a serious state of pain and exhaustion. The previous 20 km against the tide had nearly broken my spirit, and without the pit stop at the bright lights of Wisemans Ferry for hot food and coffee, I might not have been able to continue. I wouldn't have been alone, since close to 50 able-bodied paddlers had already pulled out, and they didn't have to worry about pain from once seriously broken bones.

The lights and laughing voices faded into the distance as I continued down the river, keeping away from the banks. Visibility was rapidly dropping to zero. The only way to see other competitors was the soft glow of Cyalumes attached to each paddler's kayak, dancing in the distance like fireflies. For a slower paddler like me, these distant beacons slowly dropped out as their paddlers moved ahead at greater speed, disappearing into the hills ahead. Each extinguished Cyalume added to my loneliness, and turned my thoughts to the constant pain.

Off to my right a sole paddler kept a close track to the bank, trying to benefit from the shorter distance and reduced tidal effects. This route had a number of risks that I had deemed too dangerous – overhanging trees, darkened jetties and moored boats to name a few. It wasn't long until the paddler discovered a new one, in the form of ferry cables, hanging at head height across the water. The metallic twang of impact was followed immediately by a cry of pain as the thickened garrotte made its best attempt to decapitate him. I stopped paddling and called out to offer help, but was met with a feeble, 'I'm okay mate, just a bit shaken!' This was no paddle for the faint of heart, and he pushed on behind me down the river.

The ache building up in my pelvis had caused me to take my first batch of painkillers, but their only effect was to amplify my fatigue. The pain mounted and added its weight to blistered palms and pressure sores developing on my hips. At least the general fatigue dulled the pain.

As time and kilometres went by, I started to experience a new problem. Drowsiness was leading to instances of 'the long blink', the moment when your eyes slowly shut as you're about to drift off to sleep. My arms would involuntarily stop and lay my paddle in my lap, my head would bow and I'd drift off to sleep. As I did, my balance would falter, I would start to lean towards the edge of the kayak, and it would begin to roll. The toppling sensation would wake me with a start, I'd throw the paddle down on the water to stop myself falling in, raising my heartbeat to painful levels as I'd regain equilibrium. Then it would all happen again.

The need to go to the toilet was also increasing. At my mid-way pit stop I'd made a rookie mistake by guzzling three cups of strong hot coffee, and was now suffering from its diuretic effects. Over the next several hours I needed to stop for a toilet break over a dozen times, not only slowing my overall pace but adding to the growing list of discomforts.

At around the 4.30 a.m. point, I started to suffer what I thought were hallucinations. The bow wake running from the nose of my kayak was glowing like two waving ribbons in the dark, and as I dipped each paddle blade into the water an explosion of illuminated spray burst up out of the river. This was caused by phosphorescent algae, but the mesmerising effect it was having was dream-like and magical. It didn't help me stay awake, though, and I continued to doze off.

During these confused and painful hours I started to think about the important things in life. My two beautiful little daughters, Grace and Ella, both under four, showed me an uncompromising and pure love. Their addition to my life had changed the way I thought. I considered life's risks far more seriously now, weighing up each potential activity to ensure I would stay alive for my girls.

And of course my wonderful wife Rebecca, who had not only gifted me with her hand in marriage and my two little daughters, but who had been with me in the very darkest of hours, willing me to survive against ridiculous odds with her constant presence and love. It was she who had underpinned my very survival after the horror car accident four years earlier.

As the pain of the marathon paddle increased, I thought about the long road that had got me here, to the middle of the Hawkesbury River, my battered body squeezed into a kayak at 4.30 in the morning.

Chapter 1
Awakening

IT IS HARD TO IMAGINE THE EXPERIENCE OF WAKING from a coma. Some might imagine it is a gentle, peaceful slide into consciousness, but as awareness crept back into my morphine-filled body, the first sensation was raw jolting terror at not being able to breathe because of the tube forced down my throat and into my lungs.

Without knowing where I was or why, the fight or flight reflex kicked in. Flailing with both hands, I tried to yank the tube out. The Intensive Care Unit nurse reacted immediately, pouncing on me to force my arms back down to my sides, not an easy task with a 120 kg rugby front rower. My wife spoke urgently in my ear to calm me down, until her words painted a picture I could understand. She explained patiently that I'd been in a car accident and I was on life support.

The sedation helped me to relax a little. Given a pen and paper, I was able to scrawl a few notes to my wife. Were she and our unborn baby okay? Did my father know? Was I going to die? Then, to my wife's surprise, I joked about how good the drugs were.

As I tried to make sense of the situation, my opiate-addled view of the ICU was far from the reality of the antiseptic suite full of life-supporting machines. In my mind, the room was a darkened library in an old manor, with dusty soft chesterfield couches and shelves of leather-bound books. This calming image, far removed from the stark white reality of this most desperate of wards, kept me from the panic I'd experienced when first waking up.

Over the following morning consciousness ebbed and flowed. My worried wife was asked to leave and was led to a waiting bay, while the nurse explained carefully to me that it was time to remove the respirator from my lungs. The task was complicated by layers of mucus that had formed around the snaking tube. Removal can shed these layers into the lungs, causing them to collapse and ultimately leading to respiratory failure. The only safe way to do this was to remove the tube a fraction at a time, pausing to pass a suction tube into the lungs to clean the debris, centimetre by agonising centimetre. This whole episode seemed to take hours of mind-bending agony, as I was slowly vacuumed from within. Shortly after, or possibly even during the procedure, I passed out.

I woke in the abdominal ward with five other patients. On the first day I was kept on a self-medicating morphine drip which kept me in a constant state of blissful stupor. A day later, they took me off morphine and gave me the hospital's version of heroin, a strong painkiller known as Endone. This drug has a number of common side effects, but I managed to experience one of the rarer ones – vivid and horrifying hallucinations.

During a visit by friends from my rugby team, I watched in terror as hordes of brightly-coloured monsters climbed in through the window above my bed and began to slowly devour my friends, starting with their heads. The monsters sat on the edge of my hospital bed and slowly chewed away, as if casually munching on a chicken bone. I didn't know what was real and what was imagined. My fear grew so strong that I refused to take any more of the medication.

This brought me face to face with a terrible new world, a world of agonising pain and sleep deprivation.

By now I was starting to comprehend some of the damage that had been done to me. My pelvis was utterly smashed. Not just broken, but shattered in three different areas. Part of my pelvis had torn through my bladder, leaving a gaping hole that required catheterisation. A number of blood-filled tubes emerged from various holes in my abdomen, draining blood and other nasty liquids from my internal injuries. A great wound across my side was double stitched with its own drains, evidence of a 'penetration wound' that had required emergency surgery.

The full injury list would not be made clear to me until months later. I'd also suffered a fractured sacrum, a broken rib, contusions to my left kidney and adrenal gland, a bruised lung, a bruised heart and many other soft tissue injuries. A head and neck injury was visible, with damage unknown. Unidentifiable nerve damage had caused acute sensitivity in my lower leg, leaving my right foot in permanent pain. I also had minor wounds on my arms and legs that had been hurriedly sutured.

Of all the injuries, the penetrating wound in my side was the most serious. The car I had been in was an old Morgan, a beautiful hand-made British sports car with a chassis and frame fashioned from timber. Part of the timber framing had speared through my flank, leaving splinters of timber and strips of seat-leather inside my abdomen. Apart from the physical damage of being impaled, the bigger danger was the infections it had introduced. The numerous drains running to bags beside my bed were testament to the problems I was facing, as the large wound exposed my organs and body cavities to a host of potentially fatal microbes.

By far the worst problem was my pulverised pelvis. The whole body hinges off this major bone structure, and every movement, breath, sneeze, cough or twitch is felt immediately in this area. To put it simply, everything I did caused monumental levels of pain to shoot through my nervous system.

With my outright refusal to take Endone due to the hallucinations, I was limited to less potent analgesics such as Tramadol and general paracetamol. These barely took the edge off the acute pelvic pain, making sleep impossible. I tried to trick the nurses into increasing the frequency of my dosage and secretly stockpiled extra tablets for moments when the pain got really tough.

As the days passed, my mental state declined through sleep deprivation. On one occasion, a psychologist arrived to discuss my suicidal desires, which seemed strange because I didn't recall having any. According to the daily nurse reports, it was something I had been threatening on a fairly frequent basis. The psychologist asked me about my family life, my relationships with my parents and a whole range of standard psych questions which quickly led me to point out in clear terms that the only bloody problem was the fact I was in pain every day. To get rid of him, I agreed to take the dreaded Endone at night so I could at least get some sleep.

Two to three hours of sleep at night went some way to alleviating the sleep deprivation, but it barely tempered my daily waking agony. My bed was a special moving air and foam mattress that shifted the pressure points constantly, and this helped distribute the pain. However, occasionally, after returning from one of my many daily travels to various testing stations within the hospital, the nurses would forget to plug in the bed. After an hour or so, the batteries would run down, the bed would stop moving, and the air would empty out. When this happened it felt like lying on a bed of railway sleepers.

Another major concern was that I was a smoker. I had not been able to smoke since the accident and so, apart from the inherent grumpiness that comes with withdrawal, the inevitable quitter's cough was not too far away. I knew that coughing would be near impossible due to the acute pain it would cause to my broken rib and pelvis. A physiotherapist taught me to suppress my cough through deep breathing and concentration. This worked remarkably well, except when a drink went down the wrong way and I burst into a mind-bendingly painful coughing fit. I clutched a pillow tightly to my pelvis to try to stop its many pieces shifting under the force of the coughing, writhing around the bed in staggering levels of pain. More than once I had to be sedated afterwards.

Many of my daily medications were delivered intravenously or intramuscularly. In layman's terms, via a needle. This is not something I've ever been afraid of and to start with I was patient with my six-hourly set of shots. The nurses learned that I was a willing guinea pig for the student nursing staff and I was often the practice mannequin for their injecting education. Over time, my patience wore thin, as my hands, arms, legs and stomach started to look like those of a junkie.

I also required Heparin shots to thin my blood and so avoid blood clots. This was delivered via a tiny insulin needle and I hardly noticed it in the grand scheme of painful events. One day, however, a student nurse appeared to give me my Heparin. She took out a huge 4-cm needle to draw the medication. I wasn't too concerned as it was common to do this before replacing the injector with a finer one but this time, she plunged it deep into my thigh, as if she were sticking a meat thermometer into a roasting leg of lamb. As I arched my back and screamed, the registered nurse on duty ran over, witnessed the mistake, mumbled an apology and dragged the student nurse away. It was the last day I let students near me with sharp objects!

As the days continued I battled pain, lack of sleep, an inability to cough, a tangle of drains and tubes, concerns about my job, greater concerns about my pregnant wife, and an uncertain physical future. Worse, I had no memory of the accident that had left me so damaged, or even the days before it. As I tried to cope with the new trials each day brought, I was also desperately trying to put together the events of that fateful day and how I had managed to smash myself so completely. Different people gave me a new piece of the puzzle, and slowly I formed a picture of what had happened.

First words to Rebecca after waking in ICU

Chapter 2
When worlds collide

THE SUNNY SATURDAY MORNING WAS FULL OF promise. My wife Rebecca and I were flying to Brisbane the following weekend for a friend's wedding and typically she'd had a good whine about having nothing to wear. Ordinarily, this would have annoyed me, but not on this Saturday, since I'd used her shopping spree as leverage for an afternoon of man-movies and a BBQ with some mates later that day. I happily headed off with her to our local boutiques in Chatswood where I discovered that the only outfit that was remotely suitable just happened to be a ridiculously expensive designer dress.

Still, with my wife's retail needs met, I'd secured the pass for the rest of the day to enjoy some male bonding. As she drove off to visit friends, I awaited the arrival of Dicko, a friend who shared my passion for rugby and blokey movies. He was classically tall, dark and handsome, and oozed a natural charm.

The venue for the afternoon was Mark's friend, Scott's place. The house was actually Scott's parents' family home, where he was living while finishing the last years of his law degree. It was decked out with all manner of toys including a large screen television for our DVD viewing and, hidden away in a garage, Scott's father's pride and joy, an old restored Morgan Plus 8.

Unlike most men, I'd never really been into cars, but the closest I had to a dream car was a Morgan Roadster. These classic old-fashioned sports cars are hand made in Britain with a wooden chassis and a wide leather strap across the bonnet. They also feature a gutsy engine which allows the tiny vehicle to travel at very high speeds.

The Morgan was a labour of love for Scott's father, and when I mentioned my enthusiasm for these cars, Scott tried to start it so I could hear its engine purr. Like so many older British cars, it wouldn't start despite Scott's repeated attempts, so we left it to go upstairs and start our movie marathon.

After a few hours of war and car movies and a couple of quiet beers, we fired up the BBQ and indulged in blokey banter about the weekend's rugby. Nothing animates men like flame-grilled ribs and sausages. The three of us were laughing and generally enjoying each other's company. This was the last thing I remember.

According to Mark and Scott, Scott managed to get the Morgan started and offered to take me for a short drive around the neighbourhood. Not far from his house he took a right hand turn and gave the car a little too much gas, spinning the back wheels uncontrollably and forcing the car to slide sideways across to the wrong side of the road. The street had a long blind curve and at the exact moment we crossed to the wrong side, a car coming from the opposite direction ploughed straight into the passenger side of the Morgan.

The wreck was catastrophic. Scott was left slumped over in the driver's seat with concussion, but otherwise relatively unhurt. The same could not be said for me, however, as I'd been sitting at the exact point of impact. The little car folded in the middle with its timber framing shattered and its passenger door smashed into the cockpit. In the wreckage of the passenger seat I was pinned by a piece of timber framing that had ripped through my side and into my abdomen. Broken and bleeding, I sat in the crumpled cockpit moaning in pain.

When the paramedics arrived they had to go to serious lengths to remove me from the car. The frame had to be cut and I had to be stabilised as I had lost blood from my internal injuries. Once transferred to the ambulance, it was only a short drive to the Royal North Shore Hospital.

In the meantime, Mark was waiting for our return. The phone at Scott's house rang repeatedly and when Mark answered, it was a neighbour calling to say that the Morgan had crashed nearby. Fearing the worst, he rushed out to the street and jogged down to the accident scene to see for himself. In horror, he dialled my wife's number.

Rebecca was panic-stricken by the news but immediately raced to the hospital. I had already been rushed through emergency and she was forced to wait until she was led in to see me just before surgery. The scene was terrifying. I lay stretched out on the hospital bed attached to drips and machines, pale from shock. I was still able to talk to her through the drug haze and managed to joke as I waited for the tests and treatments to begin.

One of my only memories of this stage was an angiogram. My heartbeat was erratic, so they did an ultrasound to check how much damage my heart had sustained. Throughout the test, I joked with the doctor, telling him to forget about me and move onto something more fun, like checking out my unborn baby in my wife's belly. The medical staff had a laugh as I continued to make light of the situation, with my worried wife looking at least a little confident that my good spirits were a sign I'd be all right.

Those hopes were promptly dashed after emergency surgery. During the procedure to clean out the penetration wound my blood pressure plunged and the medical team didn't know why. With my life now hanging by a thread, they decided to put me on life support. The joking confident Sean who had gone into the operating room was not the same one that came out, and my wife was devastated when she saw me.

To add to her stress, the doctors refused to tell her whether I'd survive. They simply didn't know the cause of my crashing blood pressure. I was close to death, and they wouldn't know why for a few days. They told my wife to go home and if there was any change in my condition, she'd be called. I was led away to the ICU, and she was left to absorb the terrible events.

My condition remained critical for a few days before my vital signs started to improve. After three days in the ICU, they brought me out of the medical coma, with my wife waiting by my side. It had been the most harrowing three days of her life, but she was glad to see that despite even being on life support, I was still able to scrawl a few jokes on notepaper. The Sean she loved was still there.

Back on the ward, I became a favourite of the nursing staff. Despite my terrible injuries and pain, I tried to maintain a positive attitude, which the nurses and the other patients appreciated. I made friends with the other patients on the ward, like the lovely old lady opposite who had a razor sharp wit despite her clearly dire medical condition. I chatted to her all day, making jokes and asking about her family, reassuring her when she felt in pain, and making her days a little bit more fun. When she passed away after a few days, her son thanked me for giving her some pleasure in her last week.

It became a brutally hard pattern. The Abdominal Ward was a high turnover area with very sick people. From my moving bed, I watched as patients were brought in, only to die a few days later. It brought home the gravity of my situation. I was very seriously injured, and my future was unknown.

Outside the hospital, the world continued to turn and sometimes outside events affected me. My wife and I had recently bought a dog from a rescue home and in the days following my accident he had become very sick. Tests from the vet showed he had a terminal disease, most likely leukaemia, and my wife and I had to make the decision to have him put to sleep. This hit me hard. It was just one more burden to add to my already fragile mental state.

A little while after this news, when I was in a particularly dark mental place, my wife caught sight of a golden retriever being led around the hospital. The dog was a Delta Dog – trained canines used to raise the spirits of patients and the elderly in care. She asked for a visit and shortly afterwards I was greeted by a big hairy nose in my face and a soft paw on my bed. This seemingly trivial tender moment was a watershed. For the first time since the accident, I broke down and cried. A huge, sobbing howl at everything that had happened was finally released. From that moment, I knew that there was still beauty and joy in the world waiting for me to get back to it, I stopped feeling sorry for myself and started to think about getting out.

During my second week in hospital a new drama gripped the ward: antibiotic-resistant staph. This infection can be deadly in a hospital and can't be treated. In my ward, patients kept getting wheeled out with the disease, and cleaning staff rushed in to scrub down the vacated patient bays before new patients could enter. Five out of the six patients in my ward contracted it. I was the only one who avoided it.

Instead of moving the other patients out, they moved me into my own room for a few days. This gave me some peace and quiet, but it also removed me from people to talk to, a crucial part of my own recovery. To make matters worse, I sat up and watched the Australian rugby team play England at Twickenham, the game that became famous for the Aussies' dire capitulation in the scrum. A shattered body I could handle, but losing rugby to England was far more painful!

One of the nurses on my ward was a friendly Brazilian bloke. He was the first to notice the pain the rugby had brought on, so he brought me in a DVD box set of the epic TV series *Band of Brothers*. This series depicts the US Airborne experience during the Second World War in Europe and, despite being brutal, gave me a sense of the hardships that man was capable of dealing with. It helped strengthen my resolve to beat the injuries.

I also became fond of the ward Registrar. He had served during Australia's incursion into East Timor prior to its separation from Indonesia. He was of Chinese background but had been born and bred in Sydney and had the slow drawling accent of an Aussie farmer. Whenever he came to visit it meant there was something unpleasant to do, like taking swabs from deep inside my abdomen with eight-inch cotton-tips, or removing drain tubes from inside my abdominal cavity. He always cracked a few dry jokes as he delivered the news about whatever it was he was going to do, so I coined a nickname for him, 'The Bringer of Pain'.

He loved the name, and as soon as he'd enter my room I'd moan 'Oh no, The Bringer of Pain is here ...' to the amusement of the other patients. He'd break into a manic grin, happy that I'd found a way to make light of whatever horror he was about to inflict. Towards the end of my second week, The Bringer of Pain brought some exciting news. The hospital was going to send me home, with a nurse visiting daily to check up on me. The thought of sleeping in my own bed was almost too good to be true. I had a series of final interviews with physiotherapists, psychologists and doctors before the decision was made – it was time for me to leave.

I had no idea how much harder home was going to be. Many of the comforts of hospital which I'd grown to take for granted were no longer available. My bed at home was a standard mattress, not the mechanical air-filled bed I'd grown used to on the ward. My bathroom was a narrow shape to suit the design of our apartment and not a large, easily accessible room built for the needs of crippled patients with a pelvis in 30 pieces. And I still had a catheter, which brought with it all manner of complications. In fact, the return home was anything but ideal, as my access to painkillers was reduced and the need to be more mobile increased.

The painful process of returning home also brought with it a bad case of deja vu. I'd been in this position before.

My very first kayak in Adelaide

Chapter 3
The first crash

M Y FIRST TRIP OVERSEAS WAS FUNDED BY AN unexpected tax return. At the age of 25 I'd rarely left my home town of Adelaide, so I decided to strike out in search of a much bigger city – New York. My month-long holiday included seeing not only the Big Apple, but many of the highways and cities of New York State, as well as a side journey to Washington DC and Richmond Virginia to spend some time with an aunt and uncle I'd only met once before.

My return to Australia included a stopover in Sydney. It was like a smaller, cleaner, Aussie version of New York, and it was where I wanted to call home.

As soon as I got back to Adelaide I started planning the move. I was working in the university sector but I'd had a passion for computers since I was a child. With the dot com boom building, I figured a shift into IT would give me a springboard to get to Sydney. That meant additional study and resigning from my job. Tuition costs money and I needed lots of it. I got a job working shifts for a bank in their mortgage processing centre, a sort of white-collar factory where lowly paid staff filed in almost 24 hours a day to their battery-like cubicles and churned out the bank's documents before being ushered out through rows of turnstiles.

This job barely paid my living costs, so I took a second job as a bouncer at the hip West End nightclub Super Mild. My key role was to look good in my Hawaiian shirt and ensure that the 'right' people were admitted, backed by a seven-foot tall ex-professional basketballer named Goran. The club itself was a small, dark, smoky cocktail bar with plush booths and comfortable lounges, backed by a musical score of funk, reggae and rare groove. To me this was more than a job, it was a home away from home with great people and even greater music. I loved the place.

With the financial constraints of being a student, I sold my car and bought a brand new, more economical Vespa scooter. It was my pride and joy, a silver sparkling piece of modern art to cruise the streets in style.

Between my two jobs and study there were barely any spare hours in the day. I was single but time poor. Almost all of my time centred on playing rugby, practising judo and work. I'd work eight hours at the bank, drive to the club, park my Vespa round the back and then work another six hours on the door. At the end of my shift, I'd usually gravitate into the club for a couple of martinis and a laugh to the rhythmic score of 70s funk. If I'd had a little too much to drink I'd leave the Vespa at the club and return the following day to pick it up.

One sunny spring Sunday I'd been to lunch with old university work colleagues. Afterwards, I went to the club to retrieve the Vespa, having left it there the night before. The sun was out and the traffic low as I enjoyed the ride home up into the foothills of Adelaide, cruising the near-empty streets, enjoying the wind in my face and the feeling of freedom that comes with riding a scooter.

As I rode the final few blocks home, I noticed a car coming towards me from the opposite direction. It was acting a little erratically, so I slowed down a fraction to watch what he was doing. As we got closer, he put on his indicator to turn, and just as I reached him, he hit the gas and crossed directly into my lane.

The collision felt like slow motion. Throwing the bike to one side, I tried to evade the car by going around it. There just wasn't enough time or distance and, to my horror, we hit head on, punctuated by an enormous *crack* that sounded like a gunshot. My body launched over the car, somersaulting into the air to come down hard on the road behind. As I hit the ground my judo training came to the fore and I managed a perfect breakfall on impact, before sliding across the road and into the gutter.

The shock took time to register. As I lay in the gutter I felt staggering pain in one leg, but I'd been knocked off the scooter by a car once before and wasn't too concerned. I was more worried about lying on the road, and I tried to move to the footpath. As I tried to stand, the pain reached crippling levels and I realised something was seriously wrong.

I propped myself up on my elbows to get a better look. What I saw was confusing, because my knees seemed to be at different levels – one of them was half way down my thigh. My brain just couldn't fathom what this meant until I managed to stretch my neck a little higher, only to see that I had a second knee folded under the first. As I started to comprehend what I was seeing, I noticed that that first knee had a pointy broken bone sticking out through it. It dawned on me that I'd snapped my femur clean through and it was now poking out through my jeans.

I tried to think what to do. A bystander ran over to me holding a phone and asked if I wanted to call anyone. 'Yeah,' I spat out through gritted teeth, 'An ambulance might be an idea.' The man put a call through to emergency and then asked me if I needed to call anyone else. I gave him my father's telephone number since we were only two blocks from his house.

Fortunately, there was an ambulance base not far away and the paramedics arrived within minutes. This saved my life. Internal bleeding from the huge break was filling my leg with blood, and I'd lost litres of it as well, causing my blood pressure to drop dangerously low. The paramedics immediately hooked me up to drips and then started to ask me a few basic questions. What's my name? What day is it? Do I know what's happened? What do I weigh? I understood that the weight question would be the reference point for the amount of morphine I'd receive, so I exaggerated, to the paramedics' amusement. I was gutted that they would have to cut all my new clothes off me to administer first aid, and I begged them not to cut my shirt and jacket. Despite my pleas, they hacked my clothes away and administered the morphine, before attending to my leg.

The immediate problem was that it was folded under itself and facing the wrong way. They would need to straighten it and put it in traction, so the paramedics set up a frame around my leg with a winch at one end attached to my foot. While this was going on, my father and brother arrived. As the paramedics started to winch out my leg, I screamed in agony and begged my brother to attack them. The pain was so acute I would have said anything to make it stop.

When they finally got my leg straight, they lifted me onto the ambulance gurney. I successfully pleaded for more morphine before they moved me, screaming, into the mobile bed. Once there, they strapped me in, placed my leg in traction, and pushed me into the back of the ambulance. With my brother by my side, we took off for Royal Adelaide Hospital.

By now the morphine was making me feel pretty dreamy, and I was captivated by the floating feathers from my butchered, down-filled jacket that were now filling the air around me. I was convinced that I was going to die, and wanted to give my brother my last messages of love. 'I really love you, Adam. Tell Dad I love him and thanks for being a great father all these years. Tell Mum I love her. And tell Gabbi (my ex-girlfriend) I love her too ...' My poor brother tried to remain stoic as I uttered my last words.

When I arrived at the hospital I was given a substantial dose of morphine before going through a number of X-rays and tests in the emergency area to work out the extent of my injuries. As the tests were coming to an end, a young doctor tentatively approached and advised there was one last test he needed to do. 'As long as it doesn't involve my bum I don't care,' I mumbled through the drug haze, only to see his face drop. He actually needed to do a rectal exam to check for lower spine damage. I was joking but my security licence was in my wallet and he was terrified I might turn dangerous during this procedure! He quietly explained what he had to do. Resigned to my fate, I allowed the medical team to roll me on my side for the exam, only to hear my father yell out, 'I think he's enjoying it, son!' The doctor was perfectly safe, but I certainly had a few thoughts about hitting my father.

When the tests were done I was wheeled into a waiting area prior to the surgery on my leg. A couple of burns victims required emergency surgery, so mine was put off for several hours. The traction I was in was so painful that I'd get a morphine top-up every hour or so to keep me from screaming too much from the pain. After what seemed an eternity, I was led into theatre.

When I came to after surgery I tentatively lifted the sheets to see if my leg was still there. My relief was short-lived as I found numerous wounds stitched and dressed down my leg, with substantial injuries on my knee and shin. The biggest wound, however, was down my hip. They'd had to place a 'nail', a 47-cm hollow surgical steel rod into my femur to stabilise the break, and then cross brace it with a couple of very serious screws through my knee and hip. This major hardware, I later found, made air travel interesting, since I had what looked like a rifle barrel inside my leg!

One thigh was about three times as big as the other from all the swelling, which made physio difficult. The best way to recover from limb injuries is to exercise as much as possible. I was introduced to a machine that, when strapped to my leg, rhythmically bent and extended it to a pre-determined angle. This angle was always set just a little higher than the angle I could comfortably bend my leg, creating an agonising tool of torture that I endured for up to an hour at a time.

When I came off the machine, I had the joy of a team of student physiotherapists who manually bent and straightened my leg. I never seemed to have any relief from the pain. To make matters worse, the surgeon who had operated on me brought me the news that the injury was so substantial that it would take some work to get me walking properly again. Running was out of the question. Rugby was definitely out.

The rugby news was tough. I'd played it since I was a child and it was my one true passion. While I was in hospital my rugby team won their competition and I was stuck with the news I couldn't ever play again. The day they won their final, I promised myself that one day I would play one last half of rugby, no matter what it took, before quietly crying myself to sleep.

Within a few weeks I was home, unable to walk but able to stand for short periods of time with the aid of crutches. I was completely helpless during these early recovery days and was lucky to have unwavering support from my father, Paul, who managed his building business from home. He brought me food as well as undertaking some of the more ugly tasks, such as changing my many dressings and other, more disgusting jobs.

My biggest mental hurdle was boredom. I spent long days stuck in bed with very little to keep me entertained. One day a close friend Nat and his girlfriend Georgia came to visit and brought me packets of glow in the dark stars for the ceiling, which was really funny since I couldn't stand on the bed to apply them! I devised a way by carefully placing them sticky-side-up on the top of one my crutches, shimmying across the bed under a bare patch of ceiling, and then carefully raising it to the roof to stick the star where I wanted. Each star took ten minutes to apply, so the process ate up lots of time. When Nat and Georgia next came, my entire ceiling looked like the Milky Way, with hundreds of stars on every part of the ceiling!

Over the following few weeks I tentatively got onto my crutches and hobbled around the house until, after a few weeks, I graduated to a walking stick. My father was worried I was pushing myself too fast as the pain seemed to be getting worse, especially in my hip, and eventually he convinced me to see my surgeon about it. An MRI later and my surgeon had some more bad news for me. I had developed a condition known as avascular necrosis, or bone death.

The force of the accident had caused a slight fracture of the femoral head, the top part of the leg bone that inserts into the hip socket. The blood supply in my leg had ceased getting into this part of the bone and, as a result, the bone was dying. My increasing pain was caused by the ball slowly crumbling away, and the only treatment left open to me was a series of hip replacements for the rest of my life.

I couldn't imagine how my situation could get any worse, so I decided I had better enjoy life as much as possible while I was still relatively mobile. I returned to my banking job and, despite not finishing my studies, was able to move into an analyst role where I could hone my programming skills. I also moved into a house on the esplanade at Adelaide's

Henley Beach, where I could enjoy walks on the sand and the soothing sounds of the sea. Walking on the beach was increasingly difficult as my hip worsened, so I decided to try a sport that didn't involve walking: I bought myself a kayak.

My first kayak was a fourteen foot sit-on-top surf kayak that was almost as wide as my car but just light enough for me to be able to carry over the road to the beach. I launched through the waves and paddled up and down Adelaide's coastline, riding the small waves into the beaches and enjoying the sensation of pain-free exercise. On stormy days I took the kayak down to the nearby Henley Jetty and surfed the waves through its pylons, wiping out regularly but loving the freedom it brought me.

I enjoyed kayaking along the Adelaide shoreline but I still dreamed of moving to Sydney. My fitness was building but I still had the pins in place. If I was going to move interstate, I'd want to get them taken out first. There was a risk that if my leg was hit in another accident, the pin could bend and I'd lose the whole leg. So I took myself back to the orthopaedic surgeon to discuss my options.

During one of those visits with my surgeon, the doctors made an amazing discovery – the avascular necrosis was gone. With no explanation, the blood flow had returned to the femoral head and it had healed itself. Despite some permanent damage to the muscles of my legs, once the pins were removed, I could live a relatively normal life. I couldn't wait to get the surgical steel removed!

A week later I checked in for day surgery. The pin removal would be a small operation that would take no more than 30 minutes. When I awoke I felt like I'd been run over by a truck. The nurse informed me I'd need to stay in overnight as the surgery had not gone quite as planned. My leg bone had completely grown over the pin, and the surgeon had needed to re-break the leg in a three-hour surgery to get the hardware out. What was meant to be a minor inconvenience had me back on crutches for the next few weeks.

My recovery from the surgery was quick and as my condition improved I started to plan my big move. Around this time I met and started dating Belinda, an intelligent woman several years my junior with a shock of cropped blonde hair and a penchant for antique jewellery. She was finishing her journalism degree and working part-time in several jobs, ranging from waitressing to hosting comedy nights at a city nightclub. Her true passion was writing and, inspired by the likes of Anaïs Nin and Henry Miller, she revelled in writing about hedonism and erotica. Her personal life was dedicated to experiencing as many of life's delights, substances and sexual experiences as possible to feed her creative process. Ours was an intense but troubled relationship. Over protests from close friends, I asked her if she'd like to come to Sydney with me, to which she readily agreed.

With my medical condition now stable, I was able to make my final preparations to leave Adelaide. I was granted a reasonable compensation payout from the insurance company covering the accident, which gave me the freedom to leave my bank job. I packed all my worldly belongings in a trailer, and Belinda and I drove across the Hay Plains to the bright lights of Sydney.

30 rugby teammates will never return home

Nick O'Malley

About 200 amateur rugby union players, in town for the annual Bali Tens Tournament, were caught in Saturday night's carnage in Kuta. It is feared that more than 30 will not return home.

The players from all over the world were members of 12 expatriate clubs based in South-East Asian capitals.

Lists of the missing and dead are far from concrete, and organisers cannot even confirm how many attended the tournament.

But they know that the worst hit was the Hong Kong Football Club team, the Vandals, which has confirmed only one of its 12 members in Bali is known to have survived – supporter Polly Derby from Britain.

Ms Derby is undergoing treatment for burns in Brisbane. The man she married a month ago, Dan Miller, has not been seen since the blast.

The club's confirmed dead are Britons Clive Walton, 33, and Peter Record, 32. Two Australian members

are missing – Shane Walsh-Till and Charles Vanrenen. Journalist Glenn Schloss wrote in the *South China Morning Post*: "When the explosion went off in the Bali nightclub, the Hong Kong rugby players would have been standing there, beers in hands, big smiles, scheming and laughing."

The Vandals were drinking with members of the Singapore Cricket Club rugby team. Four of the Singapore club players are dead – including Australian expatriate David Kent, 41 – and another four are missing. None were Singapore nationals.

The Taipei Times reported that four expatriate members of the Taipei Baboons Rugby Football Club and a Taiwanese national who travelled with the team to Bali were missing. It is believed Australian James Hardman is among them.

Other teams were en route to the two clubs, where the players were to celebrate the two-day tournament. Approaching in a fleet of taxis were one of the two Jakarta teams, the ISCI Komodos. The blast killed 24-year-

old Queenslander Robert Thwaites as he left his cab. Two other Australians, a New Zealander and a Canadian are believed to have died with him. Players in the next taxi were injured.

Further away in another series of taxis were the Sydney team, the Woollahra Colleagues, close enough to feel the blast repercussion, far enough away for safety. Team captain

Lachlan Benson, 29, of Darling Point, said the team left their cabs and hunted through the debris for teammates they feared to be injured.

One by one players made their way back to their hotel, bearing an injured New Zealand woman. "We were the last back, and we saw everybody was there," said Mr Benson. "We couldn't believe it."

Survivors . . . the Woollahra Colleagues. Photo: Courtesy of Richard McGrath

Breaking news, Sydney rugby players
lucky to miss Bali bombing.

Chapter 4
Not so bloody bagus

MY FIRST SIX MONTHS IN SYDNEY FELT LIKE ONE big party. I took a job at an international law firm working in IT, which funded my weekend adventures. Belinda had an insatiable desire for excess and filled our social calendar with parties and binges of epic proportions. Sydney can be a great place to find excitement, but after a while it started to feel hollow. I hadn't really made any good friends and was losing interest in the short-term highs of the party scene. Worse, I was stacking on the weight from my sedentary lifestyle.

Belinda was doing some part-time work in a local café and one day met a big strapping rugby player in all his gear. He was from a local club, the Woollahra Colleagues, and that day was their Ladies' Day. While he tried to convince her to come with him for his own wicked reasons, she instead told him about me and my desire to play one more game. He gave her the details of the club and told her I'd be more than welcome.

My old mate Nat from Adelaide had also moved to Sydney, so I asked him if he'd be interested in getting back into rugby with me. He was keen so we dropped into the club on a Tuesday night to watch their training and get a feel for the place. What we saw was disturbing – extremely fast and fit men smashing the daylights out of each other at a pace neither of us had ever experienced before. Unknown to us was that this was the club's first grade side, the cream of the club. Had we come on the Thursday we would have seen all the fat, slow players like ourselves going through their drills in a far more relaxed manner!

Two nights later we returned, boots and gear in hand, and wandered into the clubrooms right into the middle of the coaching staff's selection meeting. The coaches all stopped talking and asked if we needed help. 'I'm after a game of footy,' I replied. 'Can I get one here?' The head coach asked what position I played. 'Slow and fat,' I replied. The coaches laughed and agreed I'd be able to play with their bottom rung team that weekend.

The following Saturday Nat and I made the drive up to the northern suburb of St Ives for our maiden game. We were standing on the sideline watching the grade above us play when one of the team's front rowers had his face stomped on and was led from the field. The team didn't have any reserve front rowers. Then the coach saw me on the sidelines, a hefty new player at the club, and decided I was a prop he could borrow.

For those who don't know rugby, at scrum time eight players from each team huddle up against each other and try to drive each other off the ball. The props are the players in the middle. Props from both teams link shoulder to shoulder, face to face, and use the combined weight of the players behind them to drive their opposition backwards into the mud. It is a confronting position, and one that involves extreme fortitude, since two packs of 800 kg drive all their force into the front rows. Consequently, props are usually squat and wide, with some rude people even suggesting they're fat. I was being asked to fill in for an injured prop, despite never having played the position before.

But the coach was desperate, so they brought out the club scrum coach, a loveable grizzled rugby front-row veteran known as Spanner, to give me a 30-second coaching session. 'Keep your back arched like this or you'll break it. When you pause before you engage at the scrum, lift your right arm out and up. Keep your head up and drive through your legs. Now get out there!'

The coach held his breath, worried he had sent me out to be crippled. As I settled in for my first scrum, he watched as I mechanically followed Spanner's instructions. Finally, we engaged, I smashed into my opposite player, and the game was on. I was back playing rugby!

I finished that game and then continued with the game I was supposed to be playing with Nat. At the end I was ecstatic, stuffing myself with a sausage sandwich and a cold beer to celebrate my return. I'd been told this day would never come, and yet here it was. To make it even sweeter, I'd fallen in love with being a front rower. My weight was actually an asset, and scrums were awesome. Props were even expected to drink more beer and eat more pies and sausages than the rest of their team mates. It was a match made in heaven.

Rugby had other benefits too. I now had a few hundred instant friends who were more interested in fitness and rugby than partying hard every night. The emptiness of the Sydney party scene was instantly replaced with the camaraderie of the rugby club. Blokes from all walks of life came together each week with their families to smash themselves on the field and socialise afterwards. For the first time, I felt Sydney was home. This was what I'd come for.

As I played more, my fitness improved. At the end of the season my team won its premiership and our club planned a tour to the Bali International Tens, a round robin tournament of modified ten-a-side rugby held in the tropical paradise of Bali. I signed up for the tour and prepared to meet teams from all over Asia in what was considered one of the most exciting rugby tournaments on the Asian Tens circuit. I'd never been to Asia, so I was beside myself with excitement at the prospect, and spent my spare time learning a little Indonesian to help me when I got there.

Bali is a beautiful island which stands out from the rest of Indonesia with its unique religion and culture. While the majority of Indonesians are Muslim, the Balinese religion is a cross between Hinduism and Buddhism, with a culture that reflects Thai and Indian influences. The people are warm, fun and honest, and cater to the hordes of Australians and other westerners who come to their island to spend money and party. Tourism is the backbone of Bali's economic prosperity, and the whole island welcomes visitors with contagious smiles and impeccable service. It is a favourite among Australian travellers.

End-of-season football tours to the island tend towards excessive drinking and debauchery, and our side was trying its best to live up to that reputation. We were there to play hard, both on and off the field, and from the second we landed the boys were off to the clubs to savour gallons of Bintang, the locally-produced beer. In the first twenty-four hours it's quite possible the island was drunk dry of beer, as at least sixteen rugby teams flew in for the tournament and made beelines for the bars. Then, in a haze of hangovers and sunburn, the teams made their way to the Grand Bali Beach Hotel in Sanur, ready to get out on the battlefield.

Playing rugby with a hangover is tough, but playing it hungover in 38 degree heat is a whole new level of tough.

Each game lasted fifteen minutes, after which the players raced back to the hotel pools to cool down. Over the space of the day I met players from teams across Asia, all in Bali to enjoy the rugby and make new friends. The hotel pools filled with burly men joking and driving up the island's GDP with excessive bar tabs. This was rugby at its finest.

At the end of the first day's play all the players hit the pool and downed a few cooling beers before heading to their rooms to prepare for the night ahead. Despite the finals the next day, all the teams were heading into Kuta to two favourite nightspots – Paddy's, a relaxed bar with a painted palm tree made of steel drums as its main courtyard feature, and the Sari Club, a tiki-style bar across the road and the biggest party spot in all of Bali.

Our team had decided to hold its Kangaroo Court before going out, a sporting tradition whereby each player has charges brought before the court and punishments levied appropriately. In my years of rugby I'd seen and dished out some horrific penalties, including snorting chilli tequila, and setting body parts on fire. On this occasion the focus was on drinking penalties and, by the time we finished, several of the lads snuck off to their rooms for a quick sleep before the night's festivities.

One of our bigger players, a tall second rower from Queensland known as 'The Doctor' had crept away for a nap. He was sleeping so soundly that as all the other rugby teams left for the bright lights of Kuta, we were unable to stir him. He simply would not wake up. Finally, he jumped up ready to party. We were going to be late, but we were on our way.

Transport in Bali is generally via Balinese taxis, known as Bemos. They are small mini-buses that only really fit three rugby players comfortably, so I jumped in one with our club scrum-doctor Spanner, and our club captain Will. Spanner had already made a serious attempt to drink every cocktail on the hotel bar list and was in jovial spirits, while Will had tried to maintain some level of responsibility by sticking mainly to beer. I was placed somewhere in between.

Spanner turned to the driver.

'Hey mate, we're off to the Sari Club for a few hundred beers!'

'Yeah, lots of Bintang, bloody bagus, eh?' he responded, laughing. In Bali almost everything is bloody bagus, meaning simply, damn good.

'Bloody bagus!' we sang in unison, as the bemo pulled away.

Our driver drove the 20 km to Kuta in typical Balinese fashion, at about 120 km per hour. He wove in and out of the traffic at breakneck speed, scaring the pants off us before slowing down at the outskirts to Kuta.

Suddenly, all hell broke loose.

The sky all around us turned orange as flames rose into the sky. Traffic was at a standstill. Our bemo was stuck not far from Paddy's and the Sari Club. Police sirens were going off everywhere, people were running past us away from whatever was going on, and our driver was getting more and more agitated. His only guess was that there might be a riot of some sort. He thought we should leave immediately.

I wanted to get out and see what was happening, but Spanner and Will convinced me to stay in the bemo with them. As our driver attempted to turn his little bus around, police and military vehicles started coming past in numbers, some heading towards the chaos, and some away from it. We still weren't sure of the severity of the incident but that changed when a black police pick-up truck pulled up alongside us, its back deck full of dead bodies.

On top of the pile was a big blond westerner lying face down, with much of his skin burnt off his naked body, exposing charred muscles and sinews. My blood ran cold as I stared at the corpse. Its size and shape resembled one of our bigger players, Woodsy. I tried to speak to Spanner and Will but my throat went dry and the words wouldn't come. Waves of nausea rolled through my stomach. Before I could recover, the truck pulled away and was gone.

This horrific sight left no doubt as to the severity of the situation. As our bemo swung away from chaotic scenes in Kuta, we tried to take stock. How would we find out what was going on? Where were our other players? What should we do to find them? We didn't have any answers, so we had the bemo driver pull into a bar some way out of Kuta to try and get some news.

No-one was more concerned about the events than the Balinese. They were frantic to get news about whatever was happening. While the driver checked with the bar manager, Spanner, Will and I tried to remain calm as we watched a fashion show in the darkened nightclub. After half an hour, rumours started to circulate around the predominantly Indonesian bar, with the term 'serangan teroris' repeatedly whispered amongst the locals. It wasn't long before we worked out that this meant 'terrorist attack'.

We handed our driver a wad of money and demanded to be returned to our hotel in Sanur. With so many players out on the town we figured it was the best rallying point and would give us a chance to count off our touring party. The hotel contained a western medical clinic and as the hospitals in the Bali capital Denpasar filled with the injured, many of the western visitors were brought to our hotel instead. As we walked into the foyer, victims were being carried through to the waiting doctors. One man in front of me was clutching a hole in his head where half his scalp had been torn off. We hustled into one of the smaller bars where other rugby players had congregated, glued to TVs showing the first streams of footage.

Slowly, our teammates joined us. Roughly an hour after our arrival, the last members of our team arrived, including Woodsy. When I saw him, and realised the corpse in the back of the police pick-up wasn't him, I had a quiet cry of relief in a corner. The other teams were feeling no such relief as they continued to wait for news of missing players, officials and girlfriends. Not one member of the Hong Kong Football Club, the Vandals, had returned to the bar.

As news streamed in, we started to put together a picture of what had happened. A terrorist had walked into Paddy's and detonated a bomb in his backpack, setting fire to the nightclub and driving its patrons into the street across the road from the Sari Club. A minute later, a white mini-van packed with 1.3 tonnes of explosives was detonated outside the Sari Club, creating a huge thermobaric explosion that damaged properties kilometres away before engulfing the Sari in a huge fireball. The explosion killed not only most of those inside, but many locals and patrons from Paddy's who were by that time in the street. A third, smaller bomb had also been detonated outside the US Embassy in Bali's capital, Denpasar. Between the three bombings, the emergency services of the small island were stretched way beyond capacity. At the same time, tourists and locals struggled to find hundreds of missing people.

The next day a terrible silence gripped the island. Tourists were quietly packing up to leave while the local Balinese were praying for peace and worrying about their own missing family members. The local TV station streamed constant uncensored footage from the bombing scene and local hospitals. Piles of twisted, burnt dismembered bodies.

Screaming burns victims lined up in hospital corridors. Sobbing Balinese wives who'd lost their husbands. Rows of smashed shopfronts from the bombs' shockwaves. Trucks full of corpses loaded with ice blocks. Hundreds of Indonesian troops were shipped into the island to manage security. There was nowhere to avoid the horror of what had happened and, as every minute passed, hope was slipping for the rugby players who had not yet returned.

As a team, we decided to stay and support the other rugby clubs who had lost people in the blast. Many clubs were to lose people, but the worst hit was the Hong Kong Football Club. Before the Vandals had gone to the Sari Club, they had all hung up their wet and dirty jumpers along my hotel room balcony. As time went on, I realised we couldn't just leave them there. I carefully folded the jerseys into a neat pile and stored them in my room, waiting to find someone from their party to return them to. Those jerseys now represented the lives of young people who had been cut down in the prime of their lives by a barbarous act of violence.

There was little we could do. Our tour captain Lachy wanted us all to stay in the resort to remain safe, but it was the last thing many of us wanted to do. Some players paired off to talk about the bombing with each other, others took off to see some more of Bali before we left, and a few headed into the main town to give blood and offer any help they could. The constant presence of armed soldiers was beginning to bother me, so I jumped on the back of a motorcycle with a local to explore the mountains of the Bali hinterland.

There was no escaping the sorrow. No matter where I went, the locals would try to give me gifts and apologise profusely for the attack. To the deeply religious Balinese, their gods had forsaken them to allow such a tragedy to happen on their island. They were devastated, both for their own future, and for the impact this terrible event would have on the lives of the guests to their homeland. Bubbling under the surface was a deep anger and hatred towards the perpetrators of the crime. I heard many locals calmly explaining that they would happily cut the heads off any terrorists they found on the island. A hastily scrawled sign in a shopfront window summed up their feelings. 'FUCK teroris, you cannot kill our Bali!'

The attack may have been aimed at westerners but, to many Balinese, it was an attack on their way of life. A group of locals I had befriended even asked me, quite seriously, if Australia would consider invading and making Bali part of Australia, since clearly we loved it so much. They had watched our troops help free East Timor from Indonesia a few years earlier and saw us as a great hope to free them.

Despite frantic calls from our families to return immediately, we stayed on and left what money we could with the locals, spending up big in the markets and restaurants, before simply giving our remaining money away to the local boys who had supported our tour with transport and supplies. With a promise to return, we made our way to the empty airport for our trip back to Sydney.

The return was hard. At the airport we were interviewed by the Australian Federal Police and our cameras and film were taken in the hunt for evidence. As we cleared customs, I was pounced on by a journalist from the local tabloid, who quickly scurried away after I told him in no uncertain terms that he should leave. I made my way back to my apartment and waiting girlfriend, to try to start my life again.

Everything had changed. I'd not experienced real depression before, but a dark depression had settled in. I couldn't sleep. I had terrifying nightmares of screaming burns victims and exploding vans. I developed an acute fear of vans in general, and couldn't bear to see one anywhere near me. Time spent in an eastern suburbs café would leave me hating all the people in it, dressed in their expensive clothes and living vacuous lives of excess, while the people of Bali were starving and wondering where their next rupiah was coming from, and the hospitals of Asia and northern Australia were still trying to keep burns victims from the bombing alive.

My rugby club offered counselling services but I failed to take them up. I was struggling with nightmares and had no desire to delve further into the turmoil and pain that was affecting me so badly. I'd tried to discuss what I'd seen with my father but he'd told me I was weak and spoilt, that the carnage of Bali was nothing compared to the destruction and death his generation had experienced in World War II. The other rugby lads seemed to be doing fine and his words rang in my head. Perhaps I *was* being weak. And yet as each day arrived, I felt an overwhelming sense of sadness and isolation.

I decided to move to the beach to try and heal myself. Belinda and I settled into a small studio apartment close to the water at Bondi Beach, and I quietly hoped that things would get better.

Things did indeed get better for Belinda, who made lots of friends with the local glamour set. Everyone was either an unemployed model or an unemployed fashion photographer. In my depressed state I despised them all, and a real divide opened between Belinda and me. It worsened when I realised she was having affairs behind my back. In a fit of rage I asked her to leave, and within the week she'd gone.

This left me in dangerous territory. Thoughts of suicide were starting to enter my head. Even worse, the lifestyle Belinda and I indulged in had left me in considerable debt. I knew I had to do something to turn myself around so I moved from my tiny studio into a bigger house in Bondi with Spanner from the rugby club, hoping his company would help me get better.

Instead of things getting better, I copped one more of life's dramas when I lost my job. My depression-fed anger and attitude had been the final straw for a boss that I'd never got along with, and he took the opportunity to force my 'redundancy'. I had little money in the bank and my life was a train wreck.

Broken businesses and
destroyed lives in the main
streets of Kuta, Bali.

Chapter 5
Getting fit and getting hitched

J OBLESS, IN DEBT, WITHOUT A GIRLFRIEND, FAT AND
depressed. At 30 years of age I had nothing to show
for my life and no prospects for the future. I felt as
low as a man could go and I had not the first idea how to
pull myself out of the depression. Spanner's solution was to
be expected from a rugby front rower: start training and
smash yourself with weights.

I joined the gym at the Hakoah Club, an enormous
Jewish community centre in South Bondi, and started a
weights program. Within weeks I was addicted, returning
every day to lift heavier and heavier weights. Over the
months that followed, I dropped almost all the fat and
stacked on a fair bit of muscle, before returning to
Colleagues for pre-season rugby training. The coaching team
were astounded by my summer transformation, and as the
football season started, I rose quickly up the grades, from
fifth to second grade.

Financially, I was still in a fair bit of trouble. Spanner had let me work as a labourer for his air-conditioning business until I found another job, but the wages barely serviced my debts, let alone cover my rent and living costs. I fell deeper into debt with Spanner himself, a situation that started to drive a wedge into our friendship. Within a few months, he asked me to move out and pay him back his money, which was difficult since I didn't have any.

Around this time my rugby mate and fellow Bali tourist, the Doctor, introduced me to an old friend of his, Rebecca. She was the sister of the Doctor's girlfriend Rachel. This cute petite brunette with deep blue eyes had a mesmerising effect on me, and I felt myself immediately drawn to her. But the introduction had come with a clear warning from my six-foot-five inch rugby mate – Rebecca must be treated with the utmost respect. The warning came with a touch of menace that suggested I'd better not ignore my imposing friend.

Despite my best attempts to gain Rebecca's attention I failed miserably until the rugby club threw its annual Colleagues Black Tie Ball, a formal affair held at the exclusive Tattersall's Club. The Doctor invited me to join his table, where he had invited no less than seven single girls, including Rebecca. His offer was too good to refuse and, dressed in my formals, I joined his table of delights.

At last Rebecca and I seemed to click. We spent the night laughing with each other and I was sure that this was the beginning of something wonderful. However there was a slight hurdle to get over – she was dating another rugby player from a rival club, the Mosman Whales. As our night of fun progressed to a nightclub in Kings Cross, he kept calling her. Finally, he came to get her. There was an incredibly uncomfortable moment when he and I sat together while Rebecca went to the ladies' room, two rivals clearly agitated by each other's presence. At the end of the night, he convinced her to share a cab back with him. I figured that was probably the end of it.

Fortunately it wasn't. We continued to date and she stopped seeing him. This culminated in one of the most brutal weekends of rugby I had experienced when we crossed Sydney Harbour to take on the Mosman Whales. My rival was playing in the same grade as the Doctor and me, and the game was frighteningly physical, especially as we kept reminding them that we'd only come to their club to steal their women. My enemy took delight in rucking the Doctor's face and both he and I answered in kind with violent face creasing of our own. By the end of the game we'd taken the points and won, but all the players went home battered, bloodied and bruised.

Over the next few months Rebecca and I continued to see each other, her love and kind heart proving the best medicine for my depression after Bali. She was proof that despite the evils of the world, there was still a place for beauty and kindness. With her love and help I was able to return to work, getting a job at Rebecca's own workplace, Ticketek. I worked hard to pay off my debts to Spanner and slowly got myself back on track.

I continued to play rugby and at the end of that season I returned with my Colleagues teammates to Bali for the anniversary of the bombing. We came with a plan to win the Bali International Tens tournament, and brought with us a big hardened team of upper grade boys ready to take on the best of the Asian expats.

The Bali we arrived in was vastly different. Abandoned resorts dotted the island, weeds growing amongst the villas and into swimming pools. The economic hardship felt by the locals since their tourism industry had collapsed could be seen everywhere. The hawkers had a more desperate and hardened edge about them, although they were grateful that westerners were at last returning. The locals we'd befriended the previous year were overjoyed at our return, and the beach bar in Sanur renamed itself the Colleagues Bar for the rugby tournament.

The football itself was far tougher than the previous year. Our first game, against a team of hardened miners from Papua New Guinea, was the most brutal. We'd come out to stamp our physical authority on the tournament, as had they. Both teams seemed to lose track of the goal of rugby (to get the ball and score) and concentrated on how hard they could smash their opposite numbers. Onlooking rugby players from across Asia started muttering that they were ready to pack up and leave if this was the standard of rugby they'd have to play. When the final whistle blew the score was nil all, and both teams cracked up laughing when we realised that perhaps we should have concentrated on actual points! The two teams limped off to have a few beers in the pool together.

The next few games were easier and by the end of the day's play we were well poised for the Cup finals the following day. Before the evening's festivities got under way, a memorial to the victims from the previous year's tournament was unveiled by the edge of the rugby field and a service was held in their honour.

The following day we returned to the field to take on a team of fit angry players from Taiwan, the Taipei Baboons. There was a bit of bad blood between us as one of their players had vandalised our signage at the beach bar the night before, so we engaged in another brutal game. Despite an incredibly close game, the Baboons came away with a fraction more points and went ahead into the grand final. They went on to lose the tournament final but acknowledged during their presentation speech that we'd been by far the hardest opposition they'd encountered all weekend.

After the tournament we spent the week exploring Bali and visiting the bombing sites. Each of us made peace with the island in our own way and most of us were able to put the horror of the previous year behind us by the time we got back.

My mental recovery continued through Rebecca's love and care. After a year of dating I popped the Big Question to her outside the Sydney Opera House. In front of thousands of revellers at the open-air Opera Bar and with a few drinks under my belt for courage, I asked her to marry me. She was quick to respond with a definitive, 'Yes!' and we started to plan out our future together.

The planning was typical of most weddings. Rebecca made all the decisions, and I tried to shirk all responsibility. In the meantime I was content, like most middle-aged men, to let my fitness slip and my waistline expand as I gently moved back down the rugby grades. After a year playing sixth grade rugby, a good mate and fellow Bali rugby tourist, Rob, asked me to come and play for a new team that would be linked to Colleagues that he had signed on to coach. That team was the Sydney Convicts, Australia's first 'gay and gay friendly' rugby side. In terms of front rowers they had a small pool of relatively green players, and Rob was keen for me to mentor them as they learnt this most noble and glorious of positions. I agreed and for what was to be my final year of football, I played alongside a great bunch of men who'd faced far more adversity than that experienced on the rugby field.

As the year progressed, Rebecca and I organised our wedding and attended rugby games and social functions with the Convicts in our spare time. In what was to be a great learning curve for us, we experienced the gay culture of Sydney's Oxford Street while enjoying considerable success on the park. Halfway through the season, we'd won every game in our division and forged a reputation as a team not to be underestimated.

At the middle of the season, it was time for the first of my two bucks nights. I was having one in Sydney with my rugby mates, and one in Adelaide with friends from my home town, spanning two weekends. The Sydney one was nothing short of horrendous, with one of the rugby club's more decadent members, who I'll call only 'Mr Irwin', organising the 'entertainment'. In front of about 80 of my mates from Colleagues and Convicts, I was humiliated and tortured by ladies of dubious profession who, while wearing less than appropriate levels of attire, proceeded to tie me up, douse me in lighter fluid and set me on fire. Thankfully, I'd had enough beer to steel me against the pain, but by the end of the show I'd suffered so much I had to immerse myself in several dozen rums to forget the trauma.

The Adelaide affair was very different. With close mate Nat from Sydney and Adelaide friends Jimmy and Ned, we all dressed in safari suits and made our way to the Waymouth Street gun range – a bunkered pistol range in the heart of the city. There, dressed like 1970s detectives, we worked our way up from .22 calibre hand guns to .44 magnums, blazing our way through hundreds of dollars in ammo in the name of fun. Following that we met up with a few dozen other lads in safari suits and commenced a pub and club crawl of epic proportions, cruising the streets of Adelaide en masse in our flares and short-sleeved jackets. By the end of the night I'd experienced the best of the city's nightlife and managed to keep myself from being set on fire. It was a fitting end to my life as a single man. I was ready to get hitched.

Our wedding day was beautiful. We'd decided to have it in Brisbane, where Rebecca's parents lived, at the St Lucia Golf Course, a beautiful public course to the south-west of the city. Rebecca looked stunning in her white dress and, in the carefully groomed rose garden in front of friends and family, we exchanged vows. Now officially Mr and Mrs Smith, we celebrated our love and commitment into the night with our loved ones.

After a few weeks' honeymooning on Queensland's Sunshine Coast, Rebecca and I departed for Sydney. I returned to the Convicts who had maintained their unbeaten run in my absence, and played out the rest of the winter season. They remained unbeaten to the end and won the competition before taking their game to a visiting team from Queensland, the Brisbane Hustlers.

The team from Brisbane had obviously decided to beat the highly rated Sydney Convicts and came out swinging. But the Convicts quickly asserted dominance, with our scrum steamrolling theirs on every feed, and our backs rampaging through their defence. I was having a blinder of a game, destroying my opposite prop at scrum time, making early belting tackles on the Hustler backs, and running up the ball at full steam into their fast but small wingers. By the end of the game the Convicts had won comfortably, and I was awarded maximum Man of the Match points for my game. I didn't know it, but it was to be my last game of rugby.

The season over, it was time to spend more quality time with my new wife. After just a few months, she announced that she was pregnant. This was both exciting and terrifying, with the implications of such a life-changing event slowly becoming clear to us both. I felt like the happiest man alive, ecstatic at the thought of fatherhood and the joy that a child would bring. Six weeks into the pregnancy we hadn't told anyone, so I made plans to spend some relaxing time with my good mate Dicko the following weekend. He suggested a catch up with one of his friends to watch some DVDs and rugby ... Little did we know how that day would turn out ...

The long road to recovery.

Chapter 6
The recovery rollercoaster

MY JOY AT RETURNING HOME AFTER TWO WEEKS in hospital was short lived. Without the harder painkillers, nursing care and custom medical equipment, life became far more difficult. My prescription painkillers were barely able to temper the agony. Every minute felt like a countdown, as I checked my watch over and over again, longing for my next set of pills.

My pelvis was still in pieces and every movement created new waves of pain, which added to my exhaustion. Despite my desire to be out of hospital, I wasn't ready to look after myself, and there was only so much I could push onto my wife. Simple tasks such as showering were so difficult and painful that I'd be left utterly exhausted, both physically and mentally. Every waking moment seemed like hell, and there just wasn't anything I could do to make it better.

I couldn't get comfortable in bed and would invariably get tangled up in my catheter night kit, which gave me additional 'storage' reserves but increased the risk of a painful rolling episode. Try to imagine two litres of fluid anchored to the floor and attached by a tube to your privates and you can see what's at stake – sudden movements result in an immediate awakening and a stream of expletives that would make my ex-navy grandfather proud!

Another problem was the wound in my side. The double stitching was so tight that it had started to cut through my skin and embed itself deep in my flesh. Not only did I have an angry-looking 15-cm wound, but there was also a series of secondary wounds above and below it. Each morning after my shower, these wounds leaked fluid and pus, making me increasingly concerned. My nurse was also starting to get worried and, a week after leaving hospital, suggested I get the stitches removed and have the area checked.

I returned to hospital and my old abdo ward for the procedure. When the nurses saw the way the stitches had hidden themselves inside wounds they refused to remove them, and called for back-up. In walked The Bringer of Pain, and I knew I was in for some fun. With a few dry jokes, he pulled out a long metal suture hook, and after telling me to bite down on something, went to work exploring my wounds, looking for missing loops of thread.

I consider myself a pretty tough man with a high pain threshold, but this was like someone stabbing me and twisting the knife inside me after each stroke, sending acute surges of pain pulsing along my spine. The sutures were difficult to find and the procedure took almost 40 minutes before The Bringer of Pain cut away the last one. As I breathed a sigh of relief, his only comment was, 'Hey mate, have a look at the floor.'

The scene below me was horrific. The white hospital lino floor was a sea of brown-yellow pus with pools of blood. Litres of the stuff had poured out of my wounds as the Bringer of Pain had been cutting away at me. He pulled out a thermometer to check for other signs of infection. My temperature was over 40 degrees, and he calmly announced I'd be checking back into the hospital with an extremely serious infection.

They hooked me up to a broad spectrum antibiotics drip and tested my discharges to identify the infection. I was rushed down to the ultrasound section where it was discovered I had two separate internal infection sites deep within my lower abdomen and in one thigh. There was no choice but to rush me in for surgery to clean out the infections. Within hours, I was under the knife.

When I awoke, a new set of drains emerged from fresh holes in my flesh. The abscesses were large and under so much pressure that during surgery, pus had shot out of my leg across the theatre and against an adjacent wall. The Bringer of Pain thought this was hilarious, and said so to any of the nurses who would listen. Jokes aside, I was lucky it had been caught because the infections were life-threatening and I'd obviously had them for several days.

I was happy to be back in hospital. I had my moving air bed, nursing care around the clock and could shower in a bathroom designed for immobilised patients. Life was still hell, but it was that little bit easier back in hospital. I was now into my fourth week after the accident and I could see light at the end of the tunnel.

At the end of that week, my infection had cleared and I could be moved out of the high-dependency abdo ward and into the recovery ward, a section of the hospital with fewer nurses and far fewer medical complications. I was sad to leave the care of the nurses I'd become friends with and, of course, The Bringer of Pain (okay, I wasn't quite so sad about that!), but figured it would only be a matter of time before I'd be well enough to return home again.

What I didn't realise was that the recovery ward was in fact Heaven's Waiting Room. When I was told I was heading there I pictured professional athletes recovering from serious sports injuries. Instead, I found it was full of elderly patients awaiting repatriation to nursing homes, and none of them were happy about it. In the bed next to me an elderly lady moaned continuously about wanting to just die. Why wouldn't they just let her die? All she wanted to do was die. Opposite me another elderly lady with dementia repeatedly defecated in her bed as a joke, filling the room with a smell that kept visitors away and made living there unbearable. When there was a new pooping episode, the nurses were so understaffed that it could take hours to get someone to attend to the mess.

So it came almost as a relief when The Bringer of Pain returned each morning to give me a check-up. My drains were like ribbons, and each day they were pulled a centimetre or so further out and pinned in place. Leaving hospital was entirely dependent on the drains being fully removed, which would take another week or so. One morning, to speed things up, I yanked them all out, and strategically placed them in the bed as if they'd 'just fallen out'. When the nurse discovered this 'accident', she called in The Bringer of Pain. With a knowing chuckle, he announced that it must indeed be time for me to head home – after a couple more tests and the removal of my catheter.

This final point was important. My bladder had been slow to heal and, as I approached the six-week mark, some serious decisions had to be made. Unknown to me, operating on an injury like mine causes so much damage that it can leave men permanently impotent and obstruct the seminal tract. Basically, it leaves men sterile. For a youngish man like myself this would have been a catastrophic outcome, so the preference is to allow the bladder to heal naturally. However, it can only be left for six weeks, and if it doesn't heal by that time, surgery becomes necessary. I'd been tested every week and the bladder had yet to prove itself. This final test at five and half weeks was crucial.

The test process was an uncomfortable affair. I was led into a room with a CT scan and a nurse removed my catheter bag and replaced it with a drip bag. Then a tracer fluid was poured back into my bladder, filling it to bursting point. The CT scan was to see if any of the tracer fluid was leaking from the bladder into the abdominal cavity. I writhed around on the bed, absolutely busting, like a mad football fan in the toilet queue at a stadium after a dozen beers! Finally, with the tests done, they took the drip off and let the fluid pour out, to my sighs of joy.

To everyone's relief, I passed the test at five and a half weeks. The excellent news was tempered by the The Bringer of Pain announcing an imminent catheter removal. Somehow, that didn't sound like fun!

My six weeks in hospital came to a close, and I was able to return home a week before Christmas. I was still in a great deal of pain but had gained mobility. I was able to get around the house a little more. Over the following weeks I slowly improved and at the three-month mark, to the surprise of my rehab officer, I decided to return to work.

This presented a whole new set of challenges. Office chairs are not designed for smashed pelvises, and I quickly discovered that I couldn't sit for any longer than 30 minutes. Of course, I couldn't stand for any longer than two or three minutes, so this meant I spent a lot time getting up and down. Work was exceedingly difficult, but I had a pregnant wife due in a few months so I gritted my teeth and worked through the pain.

Tipping the scales at a hefty 130 kg.

Chapter 7
Bad habits

THE NEXT YEAR PASSED QUICKLY. MY PELVIS TOOK A full twelve months to come back together, and even then resembled a smashed crab when viewed on X-ray. Some nerve damage in one leg left me in permanent pain, but as time passed I slowly taught myself to ignore it. As my recovery progressed, a far bigger event in my life took place – the birth of my first child, a beautiful bouncing daughter we named Grace.

Parenthood is a rollercoaster ride, but one that fills your heart with joy despite the sleep deprivation and never-ending supply of baby poo. I've had the urge to have kids since I was a teenager. For me this is what life is all about. Our daughter was fit, healthy, and had a set of lungs that could rival any passing ambulance. She was simply beautiful, and made life worth living.

Her arrival filled me with additional drive for success at work. I worked harder and for longer hours as I dragged my battered body up the corporate ladder. I was working as a web producer for an entertainment ticketing company but found myself drawn to the marketing side of the digital space and soon found myself in a new role as a digital marketing manager. I had a technical background but no marketing training, so I made the difficult decision to enrol in part-time study.

This involved classes two nights a week and every third Saturday. This was an enormous commitment on top of an increasing workload and a young family, but I felt it necessary to continue my professional development. Fuelled by cigarettes and fast food, my days were filled to overflowing with work and study, with any remaining spare time handed over to my family.

Physically, my condition was worsening. My injuries had forced me to stop playing rugby and the constant pain made any exercise involving running impossible. I'd tried to take up weights in the gym but this was also far too painful. So I gave up on sport and, over time, put on weight until I stepped on the scales at a hefty 130 kg.

A year later I graduated, exhausted, at the top of my class. I'd been promoted and was now working even longer hours than my combined work and study of the previous year. My standard working hours were approaching 80 to 100 hours a week, and my smoking, drinking and bad eating habits grew steadily worse.

My first clear warning came from a doctor assigned to assess my injuries for my compensation insurance claim. In a clinical manner, he stated that my injuries were limiting my ability to exercise and control my weight, which was leading to morbid obesity. The prognosis was a significantly reduced lifespan. The words 'significantly reduced lifespan' are confronting and, as happens with so many of life's challenges, the brain uses various mental defences. I refused to believe it, and continued with my high-stress, over-worked lifestyle.

But the truth was that I was starting to feel sick. Really sick. The smoking was getting heavier as my stress levels increased and my ability to climb a set of stairs diminished as my lungs filled with poisons. I felt bloated and lacked energy, pushing me to be ever more sedentary, which made matters worse. My additional weight put more strain on my knees and pelvis and increased my pain levels. The cycle was out of control.

When Grace was 18 months old, my wife brought another daughter into the world, a little angel we named Ella. With our two girls we'd created a wonderful family, which I enjoyed on the rare occasions I was home from work. But eating away at me was the knowledge that I was slowly killing myself with stress and a very unhealthy lifestyle, and I started to question my long working hours. But with a growing family comes growing financial pressure, and I continued for another six months before I decided I needed to get a new job.

As New Year's Eve approached, I took a hard look at my life. Career wise I was developing well. Physically, however, I was coming apart. Worse, I started noticing my daughters' careful attention when I went outside for a cigarette. This final issue bothered me the most, so I decided to give up the cancer sticks for good and found a new job in the travel industry.

Despite the pressures of the new job, a fresh start with new people was the best way to keep away from cigarettes. Not being in the smokers' crowd in the new workplace, there was no pressure to head outside for a smoke break. Before I knew it, a few months had slipped by along with the urge to smoke.

But a new problem had started to niggle at me. I began to experience chest pains. Nothing sharp or debilitating, just faint pains that would come and go, worrying me but not serious enough to see a doctor. The anxiety this was causing raised my stress levels and one day, when the pains became too uncomfortable to ignore, I made my way to a medical clinic.

My symptoms fast-tracked me into a doctor and his reaction was immediate. 'Get yourself to hospital. You're having a heart attack.' If my pulse rate had been high already, now it went through the roof. I jumped in a cab and rushed to the emergency ward, clutching a letter from my doctor. On arrival, I was thrown onto a bed and hooked up to monitoring equipment.

My fear was palpable. Yet again I was looking at an early grave.

When the tests came back, heart problems were ruled out. I was suffering from stress-induced heartburn but the doctors warned I was a prime candidate for a sudden heart attack or stroke. I was kept in hospital for most of the night as I went through a complete cycle of testing to make sure my heart was okay, before being discharged.

The events of the day had been terrifying. Since my accident, I'd been pushing myself to breaking point in the desire to get ahead and I'd been given a glimpse of where that was taking me. Watching my daughters playing together, I could see how high the stakes were. I had to do something about my health. Giving up smoking had been a great first step, but I needed to find a way of exercising that would bring me back from the brink.

My thoughts turned to kayaking. I'd used it as a means of recovery after my first accident. Perhaps it would be a good option again. I didn't have the first idea where to start or how, but I recalled that a friend of mine, Richard, had done the 400-km Murray Marathon many years earlier. Talking to him would be a good place to start.

A few weeks later, my wife and I went to dinner at Kyushu, a popular Japanese restaurant in Neutral Bay, with Richard, his wife and some friends. The men gathered at one end of the table and the women at the other, as plates of hot food were brought out. The best dish is known as pork maki, a giant spring onion wrapped in pork and cooked in a barbecue plum sauce. As we washed them down with Asahi beer, I turned the conversation at the male end of the table to our middle-aged lack of fitness. Then I asked Rich if he would be interested in taking up kayaking again.

Another friend, Milo, looked intrigued when Richard talked about his experiences competing in kayak marathons. He mentioned a 111-km race held at night under the October full moon – the Hawkesbury Canoe Classic. The event was about seven months away and I was immediately interested in it as a goal to get me exercising again. I urged the other two to join me and we ended up agreeing to take on the challenge. We'd start training immediately. After more pork maki and beer of course!

The Fat Paddler is born.

Chapter 8
Birth of the Fat Paddler

THE THREE OF US AGREED TO MEET FOR A PADDLE from The Spit the following weekend. I had a few special needs due to my injuries. I had the flexibility of a tree trunk and would suffer a fair bit of pain getting in or out of a kayak. I needed to find a boat that catered to my physical needs, and sought advice from my local kayak store.

Their advice was to start with a sit-on-top kayak, which is like a surf ski but with a wider and deeper hull. These boats are much easier to get in and out of and are favoured by kayak fishermen because they self-bail and can hold a fair bit of gear.

I found a boat that looked suitable – a 17-foot Cobra Expedition. This sleek and fast kayak looked to have the right balance of speed and ease of entry. It came with a PFD (Personal Floatation Device) and a paddle. I was set for my debut the following weekend.

When the day came, we were excited to be getting on the water. Our wives and girlfriends came for some fun on the beach while we went paddling. No-one knew what was to happen next.

Sydney had turned on a beautiful autumn day and the still azure waters of Middle Harbour looked inviting. I stood on the beach at The Spit, paddle in hand and friends by my side, ready to start this new adventure. I had seven months to prepare for a 111-km kayak marathon held at night through the New South Wales countryside. Not long, considering my lack of fitness and kayaking ability.

One of my two co-conspirators, Richard, who'd done a fair bit of paddling, had brought his own sea kayak. He'd done a number of kayak marathons before, including the Hawkesbury Classic and the 400-km Murray Marathon, but he hadn't picked up the paddle for a very long time. Of the three of us, he was the veteran.

Our other friend Milo was the kayak virgin of the group. Heavily built and carrying a little pudge like Rich and me, he'd hired a decent sized sea kayak for the morning's fun. He looked particularly uncomfortable with the paddle in his hand, viewing the calm water with trepidation.

The three of us pushed off from the beach and struck out in a southerly direction, heading for the popular harbour beach of Balmoral for a coffee. The return distance of 4 km seemed like a good start to our campaign. The water was glassy and our kayaks tracked through it easily, although

Milo seemed shaky and didn't look as if he was enjoying himself. Richard was cruising along in his beautiful boat, and I was still getting a feel for the new boat below me. As we paddled past the opposite beach, we could just make out the small figures of our wives and girlfriends waving.

Middle Harbour was calm but the approach to Balmoral Beach passes a part of the harbour that is in the path of an ocean swell coming through Sydney Heads. That day, there was hardly any swell, just enough to send slow one-foot waves rolling in. Without warning, one of these gentle little bumps took my kayak side on and promptly rolled me into the drink.

I hadn't considered anything like this happening, and had not the first idea how to get back on to my boat. Scrabbling at the kayak, I tried to heave myself back onto the deck, only to have the kayak roll with me, dropping me back into the water. No matter what I tried to do, I couldn't get back on.

The two other paddlers had gone on ahead, oblivious to the watery struggle behind them, but eventually Richard cast a look back and saw I was in trouble. Milo was still struggling to control his kayak so Richard directed him to keep going while he turned back to give me a hand.

Richard pulled up alongside my kayak and with him holding on to it tightly, I was able to heave myself back on board. The boat was now full of water and, to my astonishment, I discovered the drain had been filled in with car bog by its previous owner. I had no way to empty it out, and with a cockpit full of water, the kayak was even more unstable. As Richard pulled away, I rolled straight back into the water.

Richard came back around and again helped me get back onto my boat. Once more, when he left I toppled back into the harbour. But now Richard had a new problem. Milo had also fallen out of his kayak and was desperately trying to get back in. Richard decided that he had better check on Milo, since I was swimming fairly calmly by my kayak. I wasn't really calm. Like Milo, there was one thing on my mind ... sharks.

Our fear was not unfounded. Sydney Harbour is famous for sightings of bull sharks, hammerheads and occasionally great whites. Anecdotes abound that Middle Harbour is a breeding ground for bull sharks and that the big mummies come up from its deep channels looking for food. Only a week earlier a navy diver had lost an arm and part of his leg to a bull shark during a diving exercise in the harbour. The same week, a young surfer had been attacked by a shark on Sydney's northern beaches.

There we both were, swimming in the harbour next to upturned kayaks, praying that we weren't visited by a hungry carnivore. Milo was trying so hard to climb on board that the kayak was spinning underneath him, like a big seal rolling a barrel. Out of desperate frustration, he started punching the kayak, scratching his arms in the process and spilling a few drops of blood into the harbour.

There are many risks when rescuing a panicking swimmer, and Richard was about to discover one of them. As he pulled up to Milo to offer help, he too was rolled into the water by Milo's flailing. Now all three of us were swimming in the shark-infested waters of Sydney Harbour, no more than a kilometre from where we started. What had begun as a gentle paddle had ended as a not-so-gentle swim.

After what seemed like hours I managed to pull myself up onto the deck and lie across the kayak like a surfboard. This was the only way to keep it stable enough to stay on board. As I lay there, prone, floating into the shipping channel, Milo and Richard disappeared behind a rocky headland in the direction of Balmoral. Milo had abandoned his kayak and swum towards the beach, while Richard managed to get back into his boat and tow Milo's renter into Balmoral.

As fate would have it a couple of kayakers were at nearby Chinamans Beach, having breakfast and watching the drama unfold. It became clear to them that I was in trouble, so they paddled out to offer me help.

One of the rescuers had a hand pump and I was able to pump out the water that had gathered in my boat. With my boat now more stable, I waved them off and started the slow paddle back to shore. Several strokes later I rolled out of the kayak into the drink again. The paddlers returned and helped me climb aboard. After pumping out the water again, they gave me an escort to make sure I didn't fall out once more. Just a few strokes later I fell out. I was increasingly exhausted each time. I couldn't get myself on the boat without help so, lying on my boat surf-board style, I suffered the ignominy of being towed back to shore.

The embarrassment was about to get worse. My rescuer was a surgeon who specialised in gastric-banding for the morbidly obese, and he started to lecture me on my size. As he suggested none-too-subtly that losing weight would help my kayaking, I spat back between gritted teeth that that was exactly why I was learning to paddle. I wanted to roll off into the water and drown.

But there was more to come. As the good doctor finally got me within a few metres of shore, I rolled off my kayak, expecting to be able to stand, and fell into about twelve feet of water. Coughing and spluttering, I came to the surface, thrashing in the water to get myself and my boat to the beach. As I climbed the gritty beach like a marooned sailor, half-drowned and exhausted, I was greeted by clapping and cheering from an elderly couple sitting on deckchairs. They had watched the whole thing, putting the final touch to my humiliation.

When I returned to The Spit, my wife was frantic. Richard and Milo had managed to get to the beach at Balmoral and had rung her to tell her I'd fallen off and they'd lost me. She was beside herself. After calming her down, I packed up my boat and headed off in the car to Balmoral to find my other paddle mates.

When I was a younger man I was invariably a quitter. I started five different university degrees. I worked at things so long as I found success, but the concept of working through failure was not one I grasped until my first accident. When the doctors told me I'd never be able to run or play rugby again, I swore that I would prove them wrong. It took me five long years to do so, but I learnt a valuable lesson – anything can be achieved if you persevere.

I wasn't about to let this latest failure distract me from my goal. Sure, I couldn't stay on my kayak. I wasn't really strong enough to get back on when I fell off. But if I'd learnt anything from my accidents, it's that slow progress is still progress, and if you keep plugging away you eventually get to the place you aspire to.

The following weekend Richard and I met up at the The Spit for another shot at paddling. We decided to take the calmer route up into Middle Harbour to a lovely spot called Bantry Bay, a 9 km round trip that would give us a nice workout without killing us. Milo had not returned due to business commitments. We suspected a reluctance to go through a similar ordeal, but Richard and I were still enthused about taking on the Classic and about the training we needed to do.

This paddle was totally different from the previous week's. With water like glass, we cruised our way past

Sydney's affluent harbourside suburbs until we reached Bantry Bay. The bay is topped with lush mangroves to its north and is the home to a pair of white-bellied sea eagles. It is a popular anchoring point for pleasure cruisers looking for an overnight stop. It is also the place I discovered the coffee boat.

While Rich and I took a breather, a little gold tugboat put-putted into Bantry Bay. It looked like a bathtub with a small tower of gold on top. As it stopped next to a nearby yacht, we could see it was a floating espresso machine. After the brief stop at the cruiser, the tug pulled away and slowly made its way to us.

The captain of the Coffee Boat looked like your typical old salt. With a white beard, weathered jacket and a sailor's hat, he could have come straight from a Moby Dick picture book. But one thing was for sure – he made a sensational cup of coffee!

Now our training was taking a little deviation. With the hot creamy coffee swirling inside me, I started to enjoy my surroundings and just being on the water. I worried less about balance and instead filled my lungs with fresh morning air. I felt better than I had in years. I felt ... alive.

By the third week, paddling was morphing from a personal fitness goal into a weekly meditation. I was experiencing the harbour in a way that touched me more than any other sporting endeavour. As I worked my way across the waterways, breathing in the salty air and feeling the wind and rain in my face, I was given much needed time to reflect on life, love, work and family.

As part of working towards my goal, I wanted to document the process and use it to help raise funds for the charity component of the Hawkesbury Classic. I had a neglected marketing blog which I duplicated to create my paddling blog, but I needed to create a brand around my misadventures which would be both memorable and positive while maintaining a self-deprecating edge. A name that related to paddling but made fun of my less-than-skilful efforts. Something that was simple but described what I was about. A name that would make people laugh. And so FatPaddler.com was born.

For the next few weeks I continued to paddle, exploring different parts of Sydney's waterways each time I got out in the kayak. I discovered turtles in Sydney's Lane Cove River, saw stingrays in Middle Harbour, and experienced amazing sunrises on the Hawkesbury River. I documented my days paddling on the website, lacing my observations with anecdotes about my personal failings and experiences.

Over that first month, my paddling fitness started to build and my enthusiasm for hitting the sea air increased. The early morning starts meant that I couldn't afford to have a few drinks the night before, so social drinks with friends became a casualty of the paddling. Around this time I also attempted a crash diet of meal replacement shakes and vegetables which dropped a few kilos but left me listless and unable to concentrate. With my 111-km paddle growing closer every day, I was desperate to increase my fitness and drop some more weight, so I joined a gym.

In my rugby days, the gym was a second home to me. As a front rower, I only really did a few exercises – bench presses, military presses and squats. Dozens of squats loaded with as much weight as the bar could hold. Since breaking my pelvis, I hadn't gone near a squat and had no intention of doing so. I didn't know what to do so I started with some light machine weights which did little to push me, but woke up long unused muscles. Between the paddling and the light weights, my lower back strength started to build up. I felt stronger and fitter than I had for years. Yet something was missing. Something that would push me that little bit more.

One day after a moderate workout at the gym I searched through the personal trainer board looking for a paddling specialist who might be able to help me with some tips. One of the trainers came over, introduced himself as Dirk and asked what I was looking for. I explained about the huge paddle I was embarking on and he replied that he could set me on the right path. With a handshake, we agreed to an introductory session to work through my goals, injuries and likely workout later that week.

When I returned we very carefully discussed my long list of injuries and then did an initial fitness test, which identified that I was grossly unfit and had the body of a 55-year-old. Dirk's calm demeanour was reassuring so I agreed to a once-weekly program with him to get my training going.

Dirk was an intriguing man. He was big, fit and good looking. His Afrikaans accent exposed his South African heritage, and like most big Saffers, he'd played rugby in his youth. More recently he'd been involved in martial arts and body-building, dedicating his weekends to diving and skydiving. He was always smiling and calmly spoken, which took the edge off his imposing physical presence.

I quickly discovered that behind his smiling face and softly spoken words was a sly and cunning animal. With each training session he'd start by saying something like, 'I've got a new exercise for you today. I think you're going to love it. It'll be really easy.' Then he'd smile that charming smile. One day it was squats without any weight, which to me sounded like the easiest exercise in the world. 'Just hold each one for 15 seconds,' he'd say, 'and do a hundred of them.' At ten I was laughing. By fifteen I was starting to suspect something was seriously wrong. By twenty I was in tears!

After a few weeks I started to realise I'd introduced a new Bringer of Pain into my life. For an hour each week I'd be pushed to the point of complete physical breakdown by this smiling bastard who took pleasure in my agony. To make matters worse, I couldn't stop myself from competing with

Police forensic photos at the scene of the accident.

Spanner and Sean in the bemo moments before the Bali bombing.

The game must go on

Rugby team returns for Bali tournament

By DARREN GOODSIR
DENPASAR

THERE are 27 spectators and participants missing from this year's Bali International Rugby Tens tournament, but their presence can be felt, as players dedicate their performances to the memories of friends who died last year in the Kuta nightclub attacks.

Despite terrorist warnings, 16 teams are taking part in the two-day competition.

It's a poignant turning point for many of the participants.

It was on the Saturday night after the first day of matches last year that many teams ventured to Jalan Legian, and the Sari Club, to unwind and drink away their bumps and bruises.

Lachlan Benson, 30, the skipper of the Woollahra Colleagues – the only Australian team in the competition – was a passenger in a taxi at the top of the street when the explosions ripped apart the clubs. In a twist of fate, the team had been delayed as two players, Adrian "Evil Spanner" Morris and Nicholas Love, had slept in.

On the night, many of the Colleagues raced to the other clubs – bearing witness to harrowing scenes of distress.

"We feel very fortunate compared to the other clubs," Mr Benson said. "We did not lose anyone and we feel just very lucky. Last year was our first time in the competition – but I guess you could say that we will be coming back now forever."

Four teams lost players in the tragedy, with seven Australian expatriates among those killed. Late yesterday, a simple monument was unveiled at the field, in the grounds of the Grand Bali Beach hotel in Sanur.

On it is a plaque with the names of the 27 players, girlfriends and spectators who perished.

Today, the tournament finishes, with some of the players staying on for commemoration events.

Sydney family's grief:
News Extra, page 58

AGONY: Tears flow at a ceremony held in Sanur, Bali, to remember the victims of last year's terrorist attacks.

MEMORIES: Rugby players remember those who died during the nightclub bombings.

Pictures: TAMARA DEAN

The game must go on. Sean (bottom left) at the memorial service, Sanur, Bali.

The last game of rugby, Sydney Convicts versus Brisbane Hustlers, 1995.

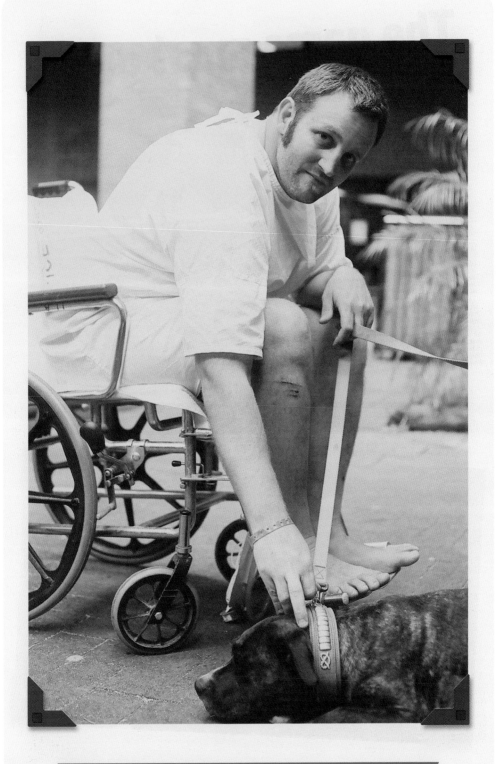

The long slow road to recovery – no mobility, no sleep, no relief.

The first attempt at kayaking with Milo and Richard at The Spit, Sydney.

Early paddling days.

▲ Paddling past icebergs, Bear Glacier Lake, Alaska.

▲ Paddling towards the face of Bear Glacier, still some 10 km away.

▲ The camp at Bear Glacier Valley.

▲ Night paddling in Chicago, city lights of the Windy City.

▲ Alaska wilderness shrouded in fog.

him. I once told him he was lucky he had never faced me on the rugby field or I would have made him cry like a little girl. He smiled and nodded, then calmly set a new exercise for me. Within minutes, I realised my gross error of judgement as every nerve in my body screamed in pain. Another time when I found him putting moisturiser on his hands, I suggested he was in fact quite pretty and had lovely girlie skin. Again he smiled, before starting me on another torturous set of exercises destined to break my body and spirit.

The training had a great effect. I wasn't losing much weight, but regular testing showed I was losing fat and stacking on lean muscle. To help further, Dirk suggested a session to look at my diet, since he was also a qualified nutritionist.

I suspect his nutrition qualifications were issued back in South Africa, because the diet he suggested consisted almost entirely of meat. For breakfast he suggested a supply of cold sausages in the fridge cooked the night before, to give me a decent protein kick as soon as I woke up. He also talked about his 'snack meal', a kilo each of beef, lamb and pork mince fried up with a few vegetables. Dirk could then have a feed of meat whenever he felt hungry, loading up on protein and skipping more starchy food like bread and pasta. This was music to my ears, until he advised the quantities I should be eating, about 15 per cent of my current meal sizes.

Over the following months I explored Sydney's waterways on the weekends and hit the gym during the week, gradually getting fitter and continuing the website with my varied adventures. I also read the book *Crossing the Ditch*, which details the extraordinary adventure faced by two Sydney men who became the first people to paddle across the Tasman Sea from Australia to New Zealand. The preparation and description of their epic paddle resonated with me, since it mimicked the journey taken by seriously injured people when they embark on a program of rehab.

A few months out from the big race I was invited to fly to my work's head office in Chicago for a conference. The all-expenses paid trip seemed like the perfect opportunity to add a little adventure of my own, so I started to plan a couple of side trips while in the USA. The first would take me down to Santa Cruz in California, a famous bohemian beach town on Monterey Bay. I'd try to get a paddle in when I hit Chicago, and then I really wanted to go somewhere to see something I'd never see in Australia – icebergs.

The trip to Santa Cruz was easy to organise. A friend I'd met online via FatPaddler.com was coming with me. Chicago would also be easy since I was already staying there. Finding icebergs was proving more difficult. After many nights of research, I settled on a trip to the wilds of Alaska.

My approaches to kayak companies in Alaska proved less than fruitful. They catered to large groups paddling tandem kayaks, staying for long periods and paying lots of money. I wanted to go alone with a guide, in a single kayak, for a couple of days, on the cheap. After trying unsuccessfully to work something out, I approached it from a different angle. Why not take my own kayak and paddle on my terms?

I approached a few online paddle friends with this problem. Chris, an English paddler living in Greenland, responded with a solution – take a folding kayak. He was preparing for an expedition around much of western Greenland in one himself, and had tested their capabilities. He was sponsored by Folbot, a US folding kayak company. I spoke to their President David AvRutick and we settled on the construction of a new Folbot Cooper, a 16-foot skin-on-frame folding kayak that fits into a large backpack. I would pick it up in San Francisco.

Now that I had a kayak, I approached the Alaska trip differently. I made my own arrangements, starting with a flight into Anchorage and a train journey into Seward, a small gateway town on the edge of the Harding Icefields. From there I would try to get into the Kenai Fjords National Park to paddle in the glacier fields there. With any luck, I would find some icebergs. From Seward, I'd need a water taxi, so I made enquiries with local businesses.

One of these businesses responded fairly quickly. The owners, a South African ornithologist named Heidi and an Alaskan guide and boat operator named Matt, offered advice on where to go and how to get about. After discussing what I was hoping to do, Heidi offered to make all my

arrangements for my five days there. With the Alaskan leg
of my journey organised, I was ready to go.

The Santa Cruz cabby with Sharon in the background.

Chapter 9
Tequila and sea lions in Santa Cruz

THE FLIGHT FROM SYDNEY TO SAN FRANCISCO TAKES thirteen hours, so I was delighted to be upgraded to business class. I was well rested by the time I landed in the US, and only slightly thrown by the fact I'd arrived six hours before I'd left – an anomaly caused by crossing time zones. Once I cleared Immigration and Customs I was met by Californian paddler Sharon.

Sharon and I had become friends through Twitter. An intense and inspiring woman, she had faced serious adversity herself, having recently come out of an abusive marriage and, some years earlier, lost a leg in a car accident. She was a graphic designer who decided in her forties to go back to university to study law, and was supporting herself by working for the Californian Department of Correctional Services. In true Australian form I upgraded her to the very Aussie monicker Shazza.

Shazz and I had organised a one-day trip to Santa Cruz where we could hire some kayaks for a paddle on Monterey Bay. The bay itself is a few hours' drive south from San Francisco, so we climbed into her convertible for the trip down. In her back seat was my Folbot kayak, which had been delivered to her house, and a case of Coopers Vintage Ale from my home town of Adelaide which she'd somehow managed to find in the US. Despite the early hour, I thought it rude not to crack one immediately as we started our drive through the eucalypt forests surrounding the city.

California is surprisingly similar to Australia. The trip down the coast could have been a drive along Australia's east coast. The other similarity was that northern California was in the grip of an enormous wildfire that was sweeping the very coast we were driving down. About half way to Santa Cruz we stopped at Davenport, a small town which had been turned into the firefighters' HQ. The town consisted of about four shops and a rocky beach. Fire trucks and news crews lined the road as flames reached into the sky above the hills just inland from the coast. Helicopters flew over the fire dumping loads of water as they tried desperately to bring it under control.

I had a more pressing need – breakfast. In Davenport I made an incredible discovery that was to become a highlight of my trip – fish tacos. The local taqueria offered a special, a couple of fish tacos and a beer for just a few dollars. I'd never heard of fish tacos but was keen to give them a try.

Within a few minutes a couple of soft tortillas piled high with mashed fish and diced tomato were placed in front of me with a cold bottle of Flat Tire Ale. The chilli sauce, called Tapatio, was piquant and sweet and I smothered the fish in it. Exquisite! Aussie tacos come in hard shells which I'd never been fond of, but these tortillas were soft and fluffy and, when combined with the delicate fish and chilli sauce, were a taste sensation. In no time I'd demolished them both and was enjoying the cold beer to finish the meal. With breakfast out of the way, we grabbed a couple of cups of what was arguably America's most disgusting coffee from a diner before setting off on the rest of our journey.

When we finally arrived in Santa Cruz I was taken by its charm. It was like a bigger version of Bondi Beach, with young backpackers mingling with surfers and retirees on the beach and in the cafes. The bay itself is stunning, edged with rocky cliffs inhabited by sea lions. Dozens of sea otters played and hunted for food among thick patches of kelp. I was to learn that a sizeable great white shark had been hunting these waters just the day before!

Because I was trying to do the trip on as little money as possible, we'd booked separate rooms in a small motel and conference centre just off the main strip. The rooms were dirt cheap and I could see why. They were dark, hot and simple, but they cost next to nothing so I couldn't complain.

As I unpacked my gear, I looked out over the motel's pool. It was like a scene from a Tarantino movie – fat leathery Americans in loud swimmers drinking cocktails from pineapples, lying on sunlounges. I was pretty lightweight compared to much of the population here. It was hard to think of myself as the Fat Paddler amongst this crowd.

My first task in Santa Cruz was to work out how to put my new kayak together. I cracked open another cold beer and laid out what seemed like hundreds of pieces across the motel-room floor before reading the instructions. Over the next hour and a half I slowly pieced it together, cursing when I discovered it was longer than my room and that part of it would have to be constructed in the bathroom. Shazz could barely contain her laughter as, dripping in sweat, I slowly put it together. After 90 minutes I stood back and admired its beauty. Then I went to work taking it all apart again!

By the time I finished it was getting late so we got ready for dinner at a local Mexican restaurant. After my earlier introduction to fish tacos, I couldn't wait.

When the yellow cab arrived, I exploded in laughter. It had an enormous set of steer horns strapped to its hood, with small American flags fluttering off little flag poles on each corner of the bonnet. The driver was a crazed looking old hippy with wispy white hair and a tiny dog sitting between the front seats. He gave me a huge grin when I whipped out the camera for a couple of photos. The ride into town was hilarious, as the eccentric cab driver fired off a stream of corny jokes, keeping us laughing all the way to the restaurant. I made sure I gave him a decent tip and grabbed his phone number in case I needed a cab later that night.

The main street of Santa Cruz was buzzing. Drunk college students wandered among jugglers, fire-breathers, buskers and hawkers selling all manner of goods on the sidewalks. Bars and restaurants pumped out a steady stream of reggae and rock as their patrons knocked back cocktails and beers. Nestled in the centre of the buzz was our restaurant.

When we arrived, two people were sitting at our table. They turned out to be Shazz's aunt and uncle, Judy and Gregg. She had organised this surprise dinner so that I could meet some of her family. To settle in, we did the only thing you can do in a Mexican restaurant in Santa Cruz. We ordered shots of tequila.

Judy and Gregg were both lovely people, but I felt a particular kinship with Judy. Like me, she worked in marketing and communications. She was the principal of her own PR company. Like most people in PR, she was outgoing and fun-loving, bordering on mischievous. Her razor-sharp wit, penchant for fun, and sneaky little dashes outside for cigarettes added up to a great deal of fun. Over hot prawn fajitas, we threw down tequilas with abandon.

By the end of dinner we were all fairly toasted, and decided to move on to one of the local clubs. Night had fallen but the streets were still alive with buskers. It reminded me of the boho-hippy culture of Byron Bay on Australia's east coast. At this hour, the students were in full force, dressed to impress and getting stuck into the spirits with youthful abandon.

As the night wore on, Judy and Gregg went home, leaving Shazz and me to continue drinking. Through many years playing rugby and working in media I had built up a pretty impressive capacity for alcohol, but Shazz was learning what so many other Americans learn when they drink with Aussies for the first time. We are unbeatable, and they are only human. Shazz had met me shot for shot, and was now looking a little worse for wear. As she got up to go to the bathroom, she slipped over on her crutches and I knew she'd had enough for the night, so I put in a call to the cab driver from earlier in the night to come and pick us up.

By the time we got to the hotel, Shazz was completely spent. She hobbled over to her bed and collapsed into a deep sleep. I was nowhere near done for the night and wanted a little adventure, so I asked the cabbie to show me the sights, good and seedy, that Santa Cruz had to offer.

For the next hour we drove around as he explained the town's underbelly. We saw the seaside tourist spots, the dark alleys where gangs were selling drugs, cruised past strips of prostitutes selling their wares, and back to the main strips of clubs where I ended my ride at a tequila bar. There I met some British backpackers and drank shots of tequila with them well into the night.

I awoke at 7 a.m. with a headache jack-hammering at the back of my skull. The early morning Californian heat tormented me and I moaned in a feeble attempt at redemption as I lay in a pool of my own sweat. It seemed no matter how much water I drank I couldn't rehydrate fast enough to break the vicious curse of the tequila. Worse, I knew I had to get up and prepare for the morning's paddle, a thought almost too unbearable to contemplate.

The one small mercy was that I was not alone in my hangover hell. Shazz looked like she had a bout of malaria, her skin green and clammy and her bubbly demeanour from the previous day replaced with the quiet look of a tormented soul. She too was cursing the tequila and the silly notion she'd had of trying to match drinks with an ex-rugby player, and an Australian one at that.

I felt way too sick to build my Folbot, so decided that like Shazz I'd hire a kayak at Santa Cruz Harbour. Shazz hired a plastic sit-on-top kayak, but I pressed them for something faster, settling on an oddly designed carbon Kevlar sit-on-top.

Shazz gets around well with one leg but I was struck by the struggle she had getting into a kayak. The launch spot was a moving platform of linked floats sitting on the harbour. Using her crutches was out of the question, so she slid across them on her bum before propping herself next to the kayak ready for entry. With a little help, she clambered into the kayak.

It was humbling to watch. I'd become quite absorbed with my own struggle, but I realised I was very lucky to be whole and that others live with far tougher challenges. Watching Shazz's determination brought home to me the importance of attitude and of never giving up. I felt proud to be kayaking with this tough woman.

It was my turn to get into my boat. I immediately realised the error of my decision to choose speed. The boat was tippy and, in my hungover state, I struggled to keep it steady. As we pushed off into the harbour I was able to work up considerable speed, but was terrified of falling in, particularly given the recent great white shark sightings. We pushed on through the harbour, admiring the yachts and trying to enjoy the beautiful Californian summer's day despite our splitting headaches and constant nausea.

About halfway across the harbour, I noticed a large brown lump moving slowly towards me. Once the original jolting fear that it might be a shark passed, I paddled over to see what it was. Shazz kept a little distance but as I got closer I recognised it as an old, shabby looking sea lion, forlornly floating on its side as it cruised into the harbour. The old sea lion passed inches from my kayak. The poor animal was either very old or very sick. It looked just the way I felt!

We were nearing the breakwater that marks the end of the harbour. Outside this we would officially be at sea, or at least in Monterey Bay with the sea lions, sea otters and sharks. There was some moderate wind chop which was making the water bouncy and as we passed I felt my control on the tippy kayak starting to slip. Shazz was powering out into the Bay in her stable plastic boat, heading to sea as fast as she could go. This was her first sojourn into the brine, having only ever paddled quiet lakes before. She was exhilarated as well as terrified.

I wasn't exactly sharing in her moment. Not only was the chop almost shaking me off my boat, it was making me feel seasick as well. I called out to Shazz, turned around and paddled back to the safety of the breakwater. There I took photos of the Santa Cruz lighthouse and followed a few pelicans around, admiring their brown plumage, a contrast to the black and white pelicans we see in Australia.

Eventually, Shazz turned around and paddled back into the harbour. I asked how she felt about heading back in. I was feeling way too sick to enjoy the experience and couldn't hide my pain any longer. Shazz smiled and admitted she felt the same way. So we began the slow cruise back into the harbour, paddling alongside a few more frolicking sea lions before pulling back up at the floating pontoon.

It was time to make our way back to San Francisco. As we drove up the coast in a fair bit of traffic, we saw that the wildfires had escalated overnight. Enormous plumes of flame stretched up into the sky above the hills to the east, the air was thick with acrid sooty smoke and the highway filled with people taking photos.

My last clear memory of the Californian coast was watching helicopters picking up water to dump on the fires. Eight of them cycled through, dropping down to a lake on the side of the road to fill their water reservoirs, before flying off to the nearby hills to dump their load. California already reminded me of Australia and the battle against fire made me feel even closer to home.

America's best meal?
Fish tacos in California

Chapter 10
Night paddling in the Windy City

MY NEXT DESTINATION WAS THE HOME OF JAZZ, deep dish pizza, the Blues Brothers and Al Capone. I was off to the great city of Chicago on the western shore of Lake Michigan. As a lover of jazz and blues, I was itching to get a closer look as I lugged my bags and backpack kayak through to the waiting cabs.

They call Chicago the Windy City and I could see why. As well as being blowy, the late summer weather seemed to change every five minutes – one minute sunny and hot, the next minute a thunderstorm, back to sunshine, and then a downpour. In the time it took me to travel from O'Hare Airport to the centre of Chicago, the weather must have changed eight times.

I arrived at my hotel in the heart of downtown Chicago, an area known as the Loop. I unpacked my bags and readied myself for some paddling later that day: I'd organised a sunset paddle on the Chicago River.

The unpredictable Chicago weather turned nasty, and by the afternoon a terrible electrical storm rolled into Chicago and pummelled it with torrential rain and strong winds. I couldn't see any chance of a paddle, so I practised assembling and disassembling my Folbot kayak inside the hotel room. When the weather cleared, late in the afternoon, I thought I might have a chance of getting out on the water.

I wasn't convinced that the tour would go ahead, so I left my kayak in the hotel room and caught a cab to an industrial area near the Junction, a crossing point for the Chicago River. The driver dropped me in front of a yard with dozens of kayaks laid out across the pebbly surface.

The Kayak Chicago business operates during the summer, taking people on tours of the Chicago River. Its guides are a motley crew of young, tattoo-covered, grizzled outdoors types, quick to throw wisecracks at the gaggle of beginners that front up for their tours. On my tour there were about forty other paddlers, mostly South American tourists who spoke very little English. One of the tour guides explained the details of the tour in Spanish. I picked out the best hire boat and waited for the tour to start. The guides went through a quick safety briefing before leading us down to the water to push off.

The fleet of kayaks looked impressive. A couple of us could already paddle and warmed up with a few different paddle strokes as the newer paddlers found their bearings. Many decided to opt for double kayaks, a common mistake by beginners. I tried not to laugh as these long double barges turned out of control, running into other kayaks as their twin paddlers struggled to coordinate their efforts.

With guides at the front, rear and centre of the group, we set off, heading south down the river towards the Loop in the dying afternoon light. The first few kilometres were less than scenic as we passed by industrial properties and factories. Enormous pipes poured pungent run-off directly into the river, creating a foul chemical smell and long oily slicks across the water's surface. Our less-than-glamorous start was topped off by the bloated corpse of a dead animal floating down the river. I quietly thanked myself for not bringing the Folbot down to these ghastly polluted waters.

As the sky grew darker and we moved further into the Loop, the views improved and the water seemed less toxic. Lights started to come on across the city and in the final half hour of twilight, reflected off the river like swaying lanterns to guide our way.

The group behind me were making slow progress. The Latino paddlers were struggling with their boats and seemed to spend more time crashing into each other than moving forward. Occasionally I'd see a boat spear at full speed into the stone walls of the river, almost throwing its paddlers into the dark dirty water below. I was getting frustrated at our slow pace and asked the front guide if there was any chance we could go a little faster. With a sly look he explained that as the front guide, his job was to make sure he stayed with the front paddler, and that I could go as fast as I liked. I grinned and took off, followed closely by the tattooed guide.

The two of us raced alongside the stone walls of the river, chatting about the life of a kayak guide. The guide's real passion was snowboarding. Kayaking was his summer job and his goal was to raise enough money to live on throughout the winter's snowboarding season. He was your typical adventure junkie, loving the outdoors and always searching for the next rush from his chosen sport. I envied his lifestyle.

Darkness fell over Chi-town – as the downtown past of Chicago is locally known – just as we moved into the centre of downtown. The city itself is a stunning mix of old gothic architecture and ultra-modern glass towers. With the skyline lit by the night lights of the city, it was magical. As I cruised through the busy canal I felt lucky to have been able to see this city, to still be alive to experience this urban adventure in a land so far from home. The dull ache in my pelvis reminded me how close to death I'd been and how lucky I was to be here, paddle in hand, cruising below the Windy City at night.

The front guide brought me back to the present by calling out for me to stop. We'd pulled a fair way ahead of the group and needed to let them catch up. We were at a junction with one course heading off to Lake Michigan, the other further into the southern end of the Loop. We decided to take the

Lake Michigan route. The other paddlers were still struggling with their kayaks but were laughing at the fun they were having. The sheer joy of having paddles in hand and cold water splashing into their faces was bringing the group together. The guides grinned at the rabble. Like me, they knew how much fun this sport could be.

On the way home we passed waterfront nightclubs in full swing and evaded the occasional pleasure cruiser or ferry moving up the river. It was pitch dark when we approached the original launch point.

When I got back to my hotel I discovered I'd missed the room service window, and was going to have to head out to get some food. I wandered the streets, taking in the sights and sounds of restaurants and jazz bars. There was a darker side too, with homeless men and women on every corner trying to hustle a few dollars from passers-by. Some of the hustles were excellent, as I discovered after being done for twenty bucks. But I wanted to see this side of the city, to feel a little of its underbelly here in the heart of Chicago's commercial district.

On my ramble I was joined by an elderly African-American bloke who starting giving me advice on the local bars and clubs. When I mentioned my love of jazz and blues, he sang beautiful jazz melodies and guttural ribald blues. I didn't know what had led this talented man to the streets, but I was taken by him. When the hustle for money came, I made him a deal – pick somewhere to eat and I'd shout him dinner. He readily agreed, leading me to a local Subway for a meatball sandwich and a Coke. This man was articulate, smart and charismatic. He waxed on about the history of the city, its economic strengths and weaknesses, the social issues it struggled with and the inevitable discussion of sport and his team, the Chicago Bears NFL football side.

As we left the Subway he wished me and my family good health and happiness, before smiling and singing his way down the street. This shared moment touched me more than I had expected. Life is full of adversity, and yet you meet individuals who can find and create moments of joy no matter what their circumstances.

First outing on Alaskan waters
at Resurrection Bay.

Chapter 11
Planes, trains and hungry bears

MY EXCITEMENT MOUNTED AS I BOARDED THE AIR Alaska flight for my next leg of the journey. I was off to Anchorage, home to 75 per cent of Alaska's population. This would be my first trip to a land of mountains of ice, so far removed from the beaches and harbours of eastern Australia.

As I settled into my window seat, the plane filled with American soldiers, continuing their journey to the military base at Fairbanks in the bleak Arctic desert of northern Alaska. I was penned in by two burly GIs who plonked down next to me in their fatigues, and further surrounded by more US military.

The soldier next to me was little more than a kid. He told me he'd just married his high school sweetheart, before his first posting to Fairbanks. He'd be spending three years there while his wife remained in Tennessee. The other soldiers joked that they'd all pay her a visit when they got leave, since she'd obviously be craving a man's attention, but the soldier just grinned and ignored the ribbing.

It was an interesting insight into the minds of the grunts of the world's most lethal army. They were amiable guys, joking and laughing with each other, but there was a dangerous edge to them which left me feeling uncomfortable. There was a sense that they were all desperate for action and well schooled in the art of war. They'd see none of that in Fairbanks where I was informed that, aside from the polar bears, the biggest danger they'd face would be boredom.

Our flight over Canada and the Gulf of Alaska took several hours. When the plane started its descent towards Anchorage, I peered out the window to see the Harding Icefield, a desolate mountain range of snow, ice and stone. The sun was low and the mountains were painted with orange and purple hues, creating a panorama that left all the passengers breathless. It was enormous, bleak and dangerous.

I'd booked a cheap hotel between the airport and the train station and looked forward to dinner, catching up on news, email and a few hours' sleep. When I arrived, I found the internet wasn't working, my room was damp and musty, and the facilities were bleak. The girl on the counter was nonplussed by my enquiries about the internet and more interested in her cigarette. I'd picked the worst hotel in North America.

The kitchen was closed so I left the hotel in search of a meal and some supplies. Not far away was a combined Italian and Chinese restaurant, which mixed not only its menu but its decor. I ordered a takeaway spaghetti and sat back to watch the coming and going in the carpark. Clearly, hybrids were not big sellers in the wilds of Alaska, but the cash exchanged on SUVs must have rivalled the economy of a small Pacific nation.

When my takeaway meal was ready I wandered into a gas station to get some water and a few personal supplies. Behind the bulletproof glass around the cashiers were two young, burly men, chatting excitedly about the weekend just gone. I'm not usually one to eavesdrop but the conversation was too funny to not listen in.

"I haven't had a good whupping for a few years now, but that sure was a big one last night!"

"Did you get hurt?"

"I was fine until I got smashed over the head with a barstool. Man, it was *fun* though!"

I paid for my supplies and scurried off back to my hotel room.

I was up at 3.30 a.m. and made my way to the hotel reception to wait for a shuttle to the train station. The small minivan was driven by a large bleary-eyed African American holding a huge bucket of coffee. No-one else was taking the shuttle this early, so I hopped up into the seat next to him.

The driver couldn't stop yawning and I wondered if he'd just dragged himself out of a bar somewhere. When I asked if he'd had any sleep, he shook his head as he sipped his cappuccino. He hadn't come from a bar, but from a different night job. He had eleven children to feed and needed to work all the jobs to pay the bills. But there was more. He was also a professional boxer, in fact Alaska's heavyweight boxing champion, and was training between jobs for his next big fight. He loved his kids, he loved being a fighter, and he had no complaints about how his life had panned out. He was a remarkable, inspiring man who got on with what he had to do to make ends meet, and all with a gentle smile.

The next leg of my trip was to cross the edge of Harding Icefield on the Alaska Railway, a line famous for its spectacular views of Alaska's wilderness. I was in the cheap seats, among a dozen loud retired Americans, who were heading to the town of Seward to board a cruise ship. They were joking, laughing and drinking wine at 6 in the morning.

Outside the carriage, the suburbs of Anchorage slipped away. It was the final week of summer and the urban landscape was replaced by lush green wilderness, with sloping hills butting up to distant snow-capped mountains. As we moved deeper into the wilderness, we saw the occasional moose grazing in the fields, enormous majestic animals. Then the green forest thinned and we made our way into the icy mountains, passing lakes of opaque glacial melt.

To an Australian who has barely seen snow, the landscape was so beautiful I couldn't pull myself away from the window. For hours we passed through mountain ranges and between huge glaciers winding their way through mountain peaks in the distance. It was incredible viewing. Even the loud Americans were hushed by the sheer beauty.

I arrived in Seward before lunch. The small town is a gateway to the Kenai Fjords National Park, the final stop for cruise liners heading up the Alaskan coast from Canada. It also houses the state's Maximum Security Prison. It's a linear town, only four or five blocks wide on a small strip of land between a Mount Marathon and the deep waters of a Fjord. Every Fourth of July, the town population swells to thirty thousand beer-swilling fans who cheer on the mad young men and women who risk broken legs and ankles to take on the annual race up and down the mountain. Seward's main business was tourism and, as the Alaskan summer was drawing to a close, the shops were starting to pack up.

In a fishing and camping store, I looked at the gun section. In Australia we rarely see rifles or handguns, so the armoury of a medium-sized militia on public display was almost too much to take in. Hunting rifles, semi-auto assault rifles, ceramic hand guns – all available with bait and fishing supplies!

My next stop was unplanned. I came across an internet cafe and bookstore full of young types, mostly backpackers, tapping away on laptops. What really grabbed my attention was a barista making coffee with a traditional Italian hand-plunge espresso machine. Now in all my experiences in the USA I've never had a cup of coffee that is remotely passable, so I tend not to drink it when I'm there. But this had me intrigued, so I stepped in and ordered a large cappuccino. On my first sip I'd found nirvana. Sensational coffee, possibly the best I'd ever experienced, in some tiny town in the wilds of Alaska!

I savoured my coffee and watched the people in the room. I'd come to identify locals from visitors by their hair. The young Alaskan men were fond of beards (no doubt to help keep their face warm) but the girls all had what I came to think of as the Alaskan bob, a short style with the top hair teased up and out and an emo-style fringe swished across the forehead. It was uncanny. Every Alaskan girl aged between sixteen and twenty-five had exactly the same cut, an angsty badge of honour.

My next stop was the Alaskan Sea Life Centre, where scientists study marine and bird life and visitors can get a closer view of the local fauna. There I came face to face with one of the biggest marine animals I've ever seen, a full grown stellar sea lion bull. In my younger days surfing down the south coast of Australia I'd seen seals and sea lions, but nothing on the scale of this animal. Each of its flippers was bigger than me, let alone its two-tonne body. I shuddered at the thought of kayaking near an angry animal this size.

My thoughts turned to tomorrow's trip into the wilderness. I had yet to paddle the folding kayak, and I didn't fancy taking it out into glacial waters without knowing what it was capable of. I had to get it out on the water and put it through its paces so I made a short trip out to Lowell Point, a rocky beach on Resurrection Bay a few miles south of the town. The cab driver joked that I'd picked the windiest time of day and he wasn't wrong. A good 20–30 knot wind was whipping up crashing waves and chop on the water. I organised for the cab to return three hours later, before making my way down the quiet, empty beach.

This was the closest I'd come to real wilderness. Snow-capped mountains edged the horizon and dense woodlands surrounded the beach. This was bear territory, so I was extremely nervous about being alone. I went to work on the kayak, carefully putting it together for its maiden voyage, before crossing my fingers as I attempted to launch it through the crashing waves on the beach.

The boat cut through the waves easily, and as I pushed off into the cold waters, it flexed and moved with the waves as if part of the moving water. Paddling into the bay, I enjoying the frigid splash of water hitting my face driven on strong winds and, before I knew it, I was a good 500 metres from the shore. Once I got out there I stopped and took in the world around me. Mountains, white-capped waves, and distant wilderness. Twenty metres away a lone sea otter bobbed up and down in the waves watching me, my only companion in this pristine world. I had never felt so alive, so utterly absorbed in the natural environment. This was living!

I paddled for the next hour, taking in the feel of the boat and its handling ability, before I called it a day. The test was successful, the kayak was great, and I was confident it would be able to handle the journey the next day. I'd had a taste of the Alaskan sea air and couldn't wait for tomorrow.

That night I woke with a start. Outside my room I could hear scraping and scratching. As I lay in the dark listening, the scrapes became more insistent and noisier, changing to a violent banging. I got up to have a look outside my room. The noises were coming from the back door, about ten metres down the hall. I wondered if it was a lost drunk trying to get into the hotel, but there was no cursing or slurred talking. I started to fear that it wasn't a 'who', but a 'what' trying to break down the back door. I decided that staying in my room might be best, so I locked my door and returned to bed. After ten minutes or so the scratching stopped and I eased back to sleep.

Over breakfast the following day I asked the chef about it. He, too, had woken up and checked the door, but quickly returned to his room when he realised the would-be intruder was a bear. The animal had been big enough to scare the hell out him and, like me, he'd locked himself in his room. We shared a nervous laugh.

Alaskan wilderness in the fog.

Chapter 12
Ice castles in the wilderness

M Y ALASKAN CORRESPONDENT HEIDI ARRIVED later that morning to take me down to the wharf for my boat ride into the wilderness. I packed my gear into her little car and we were off, stopping only to get some food, firewood and beer for the adventure I'd planned at a hostel at Kayakers Cove later. We unpacked by the cold waters of the marina until Heidi's husband Matt and his water taxi arrived. The gleaming aluminium craft was bright, strong and clean, with a cleared front deck for my belongings and cargo, and a small cabin for the bridge and guest seating.

The plan was for Matt to take me south-west for a couple hours before heading into the glacier fields where we would rendezvous with Ron, a local guide. Ron and I would make our final trek into the wilderness, into areas that Matt's boat wouldn't be able to follow. Heidi had assured me Ron was an older experienced guide with many years of Alaskan exploration under his belt.

Matt grabbed some other supplies as I loaded my gear on board. He was a sturdy looking man with a strong handshake and a laconic sense of humour, his eyes gleaming as he joked with the locals who were packing supplies into his boat. He quickly secured our gear on the front deck before ushering me back into the wheelhouse. Then, with a throaty gurgling from his twin engines, he backed the boat away from the marina and directed us into the bay.

Like most Alaskan men, Matt was a frontiersman and a gun-toting lover of the outdoors. His boat, the *Bayhawk*, was one of the few water taxis that could legally transport animal carcasses, and he joked about how often it would be packed high with sweet-tasting bear from one of his famous guided bear hunts through the berry-rich valleys of Resurrection Bay.

The dichotomy between his conflicting passions was never far from the surface. He spoke excitedly about the animals of the wilderness and truly loved the wildlife in his Alaska, having a particular zeal for the rich birdlife in the bay. He excitedly pointed out passing puffins as the strange horned birds flew past. His knowledge of the area was impressive, and the ride felt more like a guided tour as we motored through the rain and crashing waves into the ocean swell of the northern Pacific.

Despite trying to listen and appear engaged in his funny banter, I was mesmerised by the cold grey world around me. The dark waters of the bay were lined with steep cliff-edged mountains that rose almost vertically from the water like jagged shale fingers. The dense forest growth was lost in wispy layers of drifting fog before it hit the snow line, white mountain caps clawing at the sky. As one of the world's great wildernesses it is staggeringly beautiful, but for an Australian it was dark, mysterious, and dangerous. I wondered how many bears were in there, waiting to pounce on and kill some poor unsuspecting tourist.

Matt snapped me out of my trance as we turned out of the bay to head west. As we came around the last headland, I gasped at the emerging panorama before us. We could see the huge mountains of the Harding Icefield stretching far over the horizon. Enormous glaciers cut through the mountains, forcing their way down to the distant coastline through layers of low-lying cloud and fog. The air felt dense and cold, with freezing gusty winds biting at my skin as cold salty spray hit my face. The beauty of the Alaskan wilderness and sensory bombardment from the harsh conditions delivered a heady mix of wonder and awe. This was an ancient and deadly land, and it was where I got off.

Matt pulled the *Bayhawk* up by a rocky beach some 30 km out from the face of Bear Glacier. He found a narrow entrance and piloted the boat into a flowing river bustling and swirling behind the beach, and cruised as far up the waterway as was safe, keeping a careful eye on his depth-sounder. When we could go no further, he pointed the bow towards the beach and slowly motored up until we heard the crunching sound of impact.

Opening up the nose hatch, Matt folded a stairway down onto the rocks and we unloaded my two bags. We heard the faint drone of an outboard motor for several minutes before a small figure became visible further up the river. We could make out a raft, a simple craft with two inflatable pontoons and a mess of netting and tube frames across the top. It was my guide Ron and his guests. He pulled up a little way down the bank and helped his charges off the boat, a young pair of adventurers who had just spent some time in the glacial valley. They loaded their bags onto the *Bayhawk* and urged me to get into a drysuit.

As an antipodean paddler, a drysuit is not something I had ever worn. It was a serious piece of gear, like an ocean sailor's coverall with rubber booties and rubber gaskets on the arms and neck. Ron eased me into the rubberised outfit and helped me get the gasket over my head before showing me how to bend over to squeeze the air out of the suit – a necessity since I looked like a heavily inflated zeppelin.

It's hard to describe the discomfort of a drysuit in a manner that gives the full sensory experience. The rubber suit doesn't breathe and it is immediately lined in sweat. It becomes clammy and slippery on the inside, even as the cold outside air freezes your face and hands. The neck gasket feels like a rubber garrotte, maintaining a constant pressure as each breath fights against your crushed windpipe. I was having flashbacks to hospital and the respirator tube in my throat and struggled with the rising fear of being choked again. Not wanting my guide to see my weakness, I maintained a determined grin as I loaded my gear onto his raft.

Matt waved goodbye and slowly backed his boat down the moving stream. He was away, pushing out into the Gulf of Alaska, leaving me in the wilderness with Ron.

My guide was a tall gangly man in his fifties with a somewhat serious demeanour but, like most of the Alaskans I'd met, he had a keen sense of humour bubbling under the surface. He'd spent the best part of his life guiding throughout the many wilderness areas of Alaska and was clearly more comfortable in the wild than among people. He told me later about his passion for bears and his many thousands of interactions with them. Unlike almost every Alaskan I'd met so far, he didn't carry a gun. I didn't know if I should feel confident in Ron's ability to handle anything the wilderness threw at us or nervous that we were unarmed in such a hostile territory.

Gingerly, I climbed aboard the raft. Ron sat down in his driver's position, fired up the outboard and we were away, heading up the glacial river. Water was churning up through the mesh of the deck, washing against the bags and my drysuit, making me feel decidedly uncomfortable. The glacial meltwater was barely above freezing point, and a splash on my face or hands sent shivers through me.

As we continued up the waterway the view of the wilderness was mind-boggling in its beauty. On the right bank was new-growth forest, with its lush green spruce trees barely seven feet tall. This area had previously been under the glacier, and had only been exposed during the last 70 years as it slowly receded into the mountains. On our right was thick, tall old-growth forest; deep green trees lining the rocky faces of mountains rising above us. These mountains looked as if they'd been cut in half, testament to glacial erosion over the past few million years. The whole landscape was shrouded in layered blankets of low-lying fog. It was the most beautiful sight I had ever seen.

Ron eventually cut the engine and coasted the raft into the left bank. We jumped down onto the rocky shore and unloaded my bags. He suggested I put my folding kayak together and tie it up on the bank, ready for a paddle once we'd made camp. Then he was off, trekking up through a path barely noticeable through the trees.

For the next 30 minutes I assembled the kayak. Its aluminium frame went together quickly and I slipped the frame into its skin before fumbling with my cold fingers to tighten its tensioning system. Before long, *Tabasco* was ready for its adventure, so I tied it to a tree and scrambled over to the path that Ron had taken earlier.

On the way out, Matt had told me stories of bear hunts in this valley. The profusion of berries made the valley attractive to the large omnivores. The bear population was legendary. I hadn't the first idea what to do if I came across one, other than stand my ground and not run away. I stomped noisily along the path towards our camp in the hope my noise would scare away any bears.

When I arrived at camp my confidence in our safety took a further hit when I noticed a flimsy electric fence set up around our tents. The twin wires of the fence looked as if they could barely keep out an otter, let alone a thirteen-foot rampaging grizzly. Ron closed off the fence behind me as I entered the camp, which consisted of a couple of tents, a pile of kayak paddles, and a makeshift outhouse.

Ron set to work cooking up a quick feed for us before announcing it was time to get out on the water. Before we left I asked if our electric fence would actually stop a bear. Ron tried to stifle a laugh and admitted that a bear could easily brush the fence aside. But to put my mind at ease, he added, 'They don't really like it though ...' Not exactly reassuring!

I then discovered I'd have to walk back to my kayak alone since Ron's was tied up further upstream. With a paddle in hand and a life jacket as armour, I cautiously made my way through the woods. With each step I loudly called out to the bears that I was coming, before arriving at my boat unnerved but unmolested.

Launching the boat into the ice-cold stream was difficult in my drysuit, but after a couple of minutes' adjusting, I was strapped in and away. I had some gently flowing rapids to negotiate not far upstream but managed to pass through them unscathed and into the calmer lake beyond where Ron was waiting for me in his solid expedition sea kayak. We took off into the frigid stream looking for ice.

It didn't take long. At first there were lumps of ice as big as cars, which Ron referred to as 'bergy bits'. There were so many that they obscured everything in the distance, but I didn't care. This was the closest I'd ever been to an iceberg. The floating ice was beautiful, almost organic in its shapes, as different forces had melted intricate shapes and patterns into them. As I passed them, I'd gently run my hand over them, absorbed in this foreign environment. Ron was amused, since we had not even reached the main lake and its more substantial icebergs. But he was also quick to warn against getting too close, since rolling icebergs were a hazard.

When we reached the main part of the lake I stopped paddling to take in the view. Bear Glacier itself is nothing short of a behemoth, stretching up through the desolate mountains like an enormous blue serpent. This was the biggest structure, either natural or man-made, I had ever seen. Its size is so staggering that my mind could barely accept it as real, despite the fact it was still a good 25 km away.

It wasn't only the glacier that was huge. The icebergs on the main part of the lake were titans, many the size of ten storey buildings. Considering that only one-eighth of the iceberg is visible above the surface, their real size is frightening. Ron's earlier point about rolling icebergs now became clear. You could easily be rolled down into the depths of the glacial lake should one of these enormous icebergs roll on top of you. The waves created by such a huge piece of ice rolling would be tsunami-like. Despite their beauty, they were dangerous.

Icebergs rolled quite often. You couldn't always see them, but the sound was unmistakable. The cracking and splintering of an iceberg on the roll fired like a cannon. The artillery-like sound was terrifying, promptly followed by our spinning heads and craning necks as Ron and I looked to see how far away the event was and whether evasive action needed to be taken. Most of the time we couldn't see which iceberg was moving, since visibility was limited by the towering icebergs around us, so we just gripped our paddles and prepared for water surges. After a few minutes, we could relax and continue paddling among the icy towers.

Hours passed as we navigated through the opaque waters of the glacial lake. Finally, we emerged into clearer waters in front of the glacier itself, an enormous crumbling wall of blue ice. It looked small, until I realised we were still several kilometres from its face, which towered 30 metres or more over the water. The face was covered in fissures and ice caves that called out for exploration, despite the fact the calve-zone – the area where bits of glacier would break off and fall into – would be a deathtrap to any person or animal in its vicinity. It was magnificent in its grandeur, beauty and danger, drawing us closer to its heart across the lake.

Ron was less susceptible to its beguiling effects and shepherded me towards the eastern moraine, a deposit of rocks and silt piled high by the side of the glacier. When we reached the rocky base, he suggested we get out to stretch our legs. Little did I know that this was Alaskan code for 'hike to the top of the moraine'. Once our kayaks were tethered to some large rocks, we set off up the hill.

Due to my injuries, walking, running and hiking are all painful. A drysuit, life jacket and rubber boots added another dimension to our climb, as our boots slipped and skidded across the rocks and dirt. My pelvis was cold and aching. I longed for a comfortable bed and a hot cup of tea. Instead, I was dressed in a rubber suit and boots, climbing a pile of dirt beside an enormous river of ice in a bear-filled wilderness.

When we reached the top, the view was breathtaking. We looked down on the broken and cracked surface of the glacier as it met the lake, and could follow its route through the mountains. Far in the distance we could see two glaciers merging to form the colossus beside us. The ice was over 10,000 years old, heavily compacted and was about to end its journey in the lake below.

We arrived back at camp close to midnight, a fact I struggled to believe since I had not yet grown used to the long Alaskan summer days. While the day temperature was manageable in a drysuit, the nights grew unbearably cold. I put on every layer of clothes I'd brought with me and climbed into my sleeping bag, pulling its hood tightly over my head. For the next few hours I snatched broken sleep between uncontrollable bouts of shivering.

The folding kayak

Chapter 13
Creatures of the ice

IN THE MORNING I DISCOVERED RON WANDERING around camp in a T-shirt. He was in a jovial mood and chatted away about how warm it had been the night before and how he hadn't needed his sleeping bag. I couldn't get my head around the different experiences we'd had and wondered just how cold this place really got.

We had a hot breakfast and then climbed back into our drysuits, ready for the morning's paddling. I would be picked up in the afternoon so I wanted an early start. The weather had taken a glum turn. Dark clouds, stronger winds and steady rain beat down, with thick cloud settling low into the valley. The cold was more intense but I'd put on several layers under my drysuit and was ready to get back among the icebergs.

We took a different route, scouting around to the eastern section of the lake. This would culminate in a salmon-filled river in a lush part of the valley some 10 km away. Interestingly, all the icebergs had shifted during the night, many of them rolling, creating a completely different landscape. Ron said this was normal. It meant that every day brought something new to explore.

As we paddled through the rain and fog, the icebergs seemed to be turning a richer sapphire blue. Ron explained that the glacier was this colour due to its purity and compression and that the blue icebergs had freshly calved from their mother. Over coming days, the air and salt water would oxidise the surface and turn it white, but for a brief few days they retained this beautiful colour.

The icebergs grew bigger and our hands and faces grew colder. I loved the harsh beauty of the colder morning, but had started to struggle with the cold in my fingers and hands. I was wearing a pair of neoprene paddling gloves that I'd brought with me from Sydney, but they were holding ice-cold water against my fingers. As the morning marched on, my hands grew dangerously cold.

When we reached the end of the lake, we found ourselves in a small stream, surrounded by fine dark silt. The morning's coffee had led to a building sense of urgency for a nature stop. Pulling our kayaks up to the shore, we both struggled to climb out before sinking thigh-high in the watery silt. This was an extremely dangerous area to be getting stuck in, and we pulled ourselves out of the muck before scrabbling ashore.

On firmer ground, we went through our respective drysuit toilet rituals. It took me far longer to remove my suit and by the time I was back in the rubber outfit Ron was scouting for animal tracks. He found a couple of sets of fresh tracks a few metres from our rest stop. A small set of tracks belonged to a wolverine, and a larger set belonged to a wolf. On hearing that, I was pretty keen to get back into my kayak!

The soft silt on the stream-bank made re-entry difficult, Using my paddle like a snowshoe, I managed to slip back into *Tabasco*. In the process, I dipped my hands into the freezing water and now had a serious problem. The tips of my fingers, which had been growing colder all morning, were now bright red. I was barely able to bend them and they were extremely painful. Ron advised me to leave my gloves off and paddle fast to get the blood flowing back into them. I struck out into the lake and shot off out among the icebergs. Within five minutes my fingers began to warm a little and in another fifteen minutes they started to return to normal.

My mad paddling burst had taken me into a different part of the lake and among a new set of giant icebergs. The white and blue structures arched into the air and looked magnificent nestled in the fog. I wasn't the only one exploring them. For some time I'd had the nagging feeling that something was following me. All morning I'd heard splashes behind my kayak, but when I looked over my shoulder, could not see what was causing the disturbance. The noises seemed to be getting closer and I was getting decidedly nervous about whatever it was that was stalking me. As I looked back I noticed a small dark shape 20 metres behind me. A dark brown, furry head peered out, with huge brown eyes and little nostrils above the surface. I was being followed by a curious young seal which would swim up quite close to the kayak before diving underwater at any sign I might look at it. For the rest of the paddle this little fellow was never far behind me, watching intently before diving and resurfacing in a different area.

The innocence and enthusiasm of the curious little seal reminded me of my children. Unlike the seal swimming in the wilderness ice, my kids were probably sitting inside playing with my iPhone. My own childhood involved a lot of time outdoors and I could see how important it was that I get my kids outside too, to connect with the physical world and experience the beauty of nature. How to do this was a challenge I considered as I drifted across the frigid water.

We continued through the lake as the wind picked up and the temperature dropped. Clouds settled lower into the valley, wrapping the tops of the bergs and painting the landscape with strokes of grey. The rain continued its steady drumming on the deck of my kayak as I cruised between the ice, its hypnotic beat adding to the surreal atmosphere.

As I steered towards the edge of the lake, a low iceberg came into view. It was a beautiful blue, shimmering in the light like a sapphire. Despite the dangers of getting too close, I just had to touch this magnificent, ancient structure. I paddled close to lay my hand on its cold hard surface. It was unimaginably beautiful, floating like an ice castle freshly carved out of its mother glacier, guarding the lake and her population of seals. This was the sight I'd travelled halfway around the world for, and I wasn't disappointed.

After circling the berg a few times, we headed back to camp. Matt was picking me up in his sea taxi when the tide was high, and I needed to get back at exactly the right time for him to get his boat into the river system. Ron was going to pick up my gear from the camp and motor it back to the pick-up point. He directed me to continue until I hit the river system and then, watching the currents, paddle onward to meet Matt.

I headed off on my own down the waterway, dodging the ice and watching the coast for bears, when the current picked up. The ice bits were moving downstream at a faster pace and, looking up, I could see the telltale sign of rapids ahead. I wasn't too concerned as they were small, but I knew I was in a material 'skin on frame' kayak which might not take kindly to shooting across rocks. My concern increased when I found myself wedged in the rocks, unable to get out due to the fast-flowing current, but unable to move across the rocks. I lifted myself half out of the kayak to raise its clearance and, with a final shove, slid through to deeper water.

I continued downstream until I came to the junction with the inlet, where currents were swirling about with icy bits. I couldn't see Matt so I turned into the current away from our rendezvous and rode across the waterway to the old glacial moraine that separated the lake from the Gulf of Alaska. Climbing out of the boat, I took a good look.

It was an incredible sight. The woods where we had camped continued back for a few kilometres before opening up into the lake system. Behind them were the mountains of the Harding Icefield, enormous grey giants split apart by the wide expanse of Bear Glacier. As I followed it up into the mountains I could see where it split into the two feeder glaciers that combined to form this gigantic ice mass. Each huge feeder wandered off in different directions through the mountains.

One thing that stood out was the shape of the valley itself. The face of Bear Glacier has receded some 30 to 40 km over the last century, and I was standing on its original moraine. Many of the glaciers in Alaska have receded and it's hard to doubt that it is an effect of global warming. The view was beautiful, but I was left with a touch of sadness, wondering how long mankind had to enjoy the pristine glacial wilderness.

Just then, a little brown head popped up through the ice not far ahead, and I recognised my little seal shadow. With a laugh I waved him off. I hoped that his descendants would be swimming this lake when I was long gone.

My thoughts were interrupted by the sight of Ron's yellow motorised raft coming from one direction, and Matt's little silver boat entering the inlet from the other. I climbed back into my kayak, pushed off into the current and rode the water and ice down the stream. Ron had pulled up not far from the rapids, a good few hundred metres back against the current, and it looked like I was going to have to paddle back upstream against the icy current. I strained behind the paddle alongside Matt until he turned and beached his boat next to Ron with a crunch. Exhausted and out of breath, I pulled up a few minutes later, ready for my trip back.

Matt carried my still-assembled kayak onto the front deck and secured it, as I eased myself into a chair in his cabin. On our way back down the river and out to sea, Matt regaled me with stories of bear hunts in the valley. I stared into the rough grey seas ahead, unsure whether to be disappointed or quietly relieved not to have seen any.

A few minutes after we pulled away from the glacial lake we stumbled across a humpback whale breaching with her calf. We were still a few hundred metres off and Matt quickly turned away, explaining that he didn't want to alert the tour boats that whales were there by stopping. Despite his efforts, we heard excited chatter on the radio and within minutes a fleet of whale-watching boats steamed into the bay. The foreign-owned and captained vessels that came chasing the whales could be reckless.

Every summer a huge international worker population came to Alaska to take up jobs in bars, on boats, in shops and hotels. There was a lot of resentment from the local population because these tourist dollars were funnelled out of Alaska to the 'Lower 48' states of mainland USA. In the US, income tax is usually levied by both the federal and state governments, but Alaska has no state-based income tax, so all the wages earned by seasonal workers leave the state untaxed. Tourism is an important part of the state's economy and almost every local I talked to brought this issue up.

Matt was not happy about the tax loophole, but he was more concerned for the wildlife. Throughout our journey he played a cat-and-mouse game with the whale-watching boats, leading them into areas where he knew they'd find nothing, or to places only his custom-designed boat could go.

My destination was a cabin in the wilderness known as Kayakers Cove. This little hostel is a gateway to kayaking the entrance of Resurrection Bay. Before we got there, Matt took me out to see the last islands to the south – remote spikes of rock that rose straight up hundreds of metres from the ocean floor and took the full brunt of the ocean swell from the Pacific into the Gulf of Alaska. These bleak little land masses were homes to thousands of birds as well as small groups of Steller sea lions, all of whom were vigorously fighting over the available haul-out space. The losers of these battles fell back into the water, joining a dozen others, before the cycle started again as they tried to fight their way back to a piece of resting spot.

This was a mirror to my own struggles. The sea lions were never assured of a place to keep their head above water, fighting every day to hold a little piece of land for a short time. If they grew too weak to fight, they could not manage a place to rest and risked slipping away to fend for themselves or to die. Life often felt like that for me, and no doubt for others too. Constantly pushing myself at work, working harder and longer just to gain a little financial security was exhausting. Maybe I was even killing myself in the process. It was a bleak and depressing thought but, like the sea lions, I had my own young to feed and support, and would have to shut up and get on with it. At least, I consoled myself, I got to enjoy the Aussie sunshine!

Matt pointed to colonies of puffins that skimmed across the water looking for food. They were crazy little things, fearless towards other bigger birds, chasing off anything that came near their nests. Matt mentioned their one weakness: their landing skills. He laughed as he told me to keep an eye out for any landings.

It didn't take long. A big horned puffin swooped over the bow of the boat and turned to land alongside us. It put its feet out to land, much as a duck would, but when it hit the water, it tripped and tumbled over its own feet, bouncing across the water until it finally came to a halt, slightly ruffled but otherwise fine. It glared at us, seemingly annoyed at our laughter, before diving into the water.

It was time to leave. Matt turned the boat north again and, pausing occasionally to look at bird colonies or to hide from whale-watcher boats, headed towards the tip of the peninsula. As we approached the cove, I admired the thick green woodlands of this wilderness area, rising up to hills and mountains nestled in cloud, the woods thinning out at the top and replaced by icecaps. Matt calmly advised me there were lots of bears in this part of the wilderness, but of more interest were the creatures in the waters, since this was a common route for orca and other whales. With my mind tuned in to thoughts of predators in and out of the water, we continued the last kilometre of the journey in relative silence.

Riding out to Kayakers Cove.

Chapter 14
The cabin in the woods

MATT THROTTLED DOWN THE BOAT AS WE rounded a small headland, passing by a small island before turning into a cove of still water. I could just make out a stony ramp leading to a wooden cabin, built high, almost in the treetops. The woods were thick and rose steeply up a small mountain behind the cabin. Next to the house was a stack of single and double kayaks, and below the front deck, piles of paddles, life jackets and hand pumps.

The hostel, Kayakers Cove, was famous for hosting visiting paddlers who explored the local islands of Resurrection Bay. It was costing me the princely sum of $25 (including sleeping bag hire) and had all the comforts of home – with the exception of power, water and sewerage! I'd brought my own food, firewood, water and other supplies.

Inside, a dozen or so travellers lounged around chatting or playing cards. Most of them were from the US or Canada, but a couple of German and Swiss travellers were there too, hustling the card games and swigging away on beer. The evening looked like it was going to be fun. I added my own beer supply to the coolers placed outside the main entrance, and joined the card game.

At thirty-seven years of age this was my first experience in a hostel, and I was loving it. Here in Alaska none of the travellers were seeking a comfortable shopping holiday. This was a cabin full of adventurous souls, all stopped briefly in the one place to share stories and have a laugh before moving on to new adventures. The stories, card-playing and laughter continued as the pile of empty beer bottles grew and the light started to dip over the mountains. Shortly afterwards, I experienced one of the true horrors of the Cove.

After a few beers, I felt the need to visit nature. The cabin had a narrow wooden boardwalk that snaked out from the back door across the mountainside and ended in a little outhouse with stunning views over the bay. The toilet was simply a hole, with a long drop down to a small meandering stream that washed away somewhere into the waters below. There hadn't been much rain in the previous few weeks so the stream was still, and the pile of human waste at the bottom of the long drop created a stench that could have been bottled as a biological weapon. Gagging, I decided never to visit the toilet again, no matter how desperate I became.

I returned to the cabin and found the inhabitants each preparing their own dinner before the daylight ended. I quickly put together a meal of penne amatriciana, a pasta dish made with tomato, bacon, onion and chilli, to the bemused look of the Americans around me. Bacon in pasta was simply unheard of, and they crowded around to see the travesty I was creating. When I finished, a few brave travellers tried some of my dinner and it got the thumbs up from everyone.

By the time we'd finished our respective dinners the sun was down and the cabin was lit only by candles and the fire burning in the hearth. We continued our cards and beer drinking by the flickering light into late evening before we called it a night.

I awoke early the next day. I couldn't wait to get on the water and was the first paddler ready to go exploring. After kitting up in my warmest paddling gear, I climbed into my folding kayak and pushed off into the cold deep waters of the bay, staying close to the shoreline as I slowly paddled north.

The scenery was wild and beautiful. Thick green forest lined the shores and reflected off the still emerald water. Waterways cut into the mountains and there seemed to be an endless maze of routes to explore and enjoy. I steered my way into a steep valley, and the water became shallow as it turned into the inlet for a mountain stream. As I paddled further upstream, the water erupted as a salmon emerged from the water beside me. Then another salmon leapt out of the water, almost landing on top of the kayak. More and more of the big fish jumped around me, churning the water into a bubbling frenzy of fish. I could see the bottom of the stream and was shocked to see it littered with thousands of dead salmon, forming a carpet of fish corpses across the stream bed. Although I knew that this was due to it being spawning season and salmon drop dead after they have spawned, I was still shocked.

A frenzied chattering to my left startled me. On the stream bank between some rocks, two sea otters stood up staring at me, angrily chattering in my direction as if telling me off for invading their feeding grounds. I laughed at them but they continued their barrage of otter abuse, not letting up until I turned my kayak around and paddled back towards the open water.

I felt really blessed to be in this wilderness. There are so few places, natural or man-made, that can be experienced alone. It brought solace to my soul as I slowly made my way through this beautiful landscape with only my thoughts and the occasional salmon for company. When you have been close to losing your life, moments like these mean the most. Moments of true, unadulterated beauty. Moments where you find yourself. Moments of peace.

Towards the open waters of the bay I noticed a large species of jellyfish, similar to the giants I'd occasionally seen on the Hawkesbury River. The Sydney variety are the size of basketballs with a short stubby tail of fronds, but these Alaskan jellies were even bigger and had huge long plumes trailing behind them. I was later to find out that these Lion's Mane Jellyfish are the biggest in the world!

I made it back out into the bay and continued a little further into deeper waters. The conditions were glassy and I couldn't have hoped for a better sea state for exploration on my slow cruise towards some of the smaller islands on my way back to Kayakers Cove. As my mind drifted to thoughts of my family back home, I was swiftly brought back to reality when somewhere behind me the water erupted.

I spun around to see what was going on. There was nothing but a disturbed outline on the water's surface. Then a huge white object broke the surface about 20 metres to my right. This was followed by another eruption of water and spray. As the object slipped back under the water, yet another broke the surface even closer, again blowing off a big spray of water before sinking into the deep. By the time I realised these were not prehistoric giant killer sharks about to consume me, but some type of white dolphin or whale, they started surfacing all around my kayak, blowing off spray before slipping under the water again. I was surrounded by nine or ten of these extraordinary sea mammals and as they ventured closer to my kayak I could make out their shape.

Slightly longer than my kayak, they were sleek and white, and had backs like whales, with no dorsal fin that I could see. Their heads were bulbous and dolphin-like. As one got closer I swear I could see a smile on its face. This was a pod of beluga whales, a species I knew very little about, since they don't frequent Australian waters. Here I was in the wilderness, separated from the water by a sliver of material, and surrounded by massive sea animals.

The whales must have been curious because they stayed with me for about thirty minutes, filling the air with the pungent smell of whale breath. This was the most amazing paddling experience I'd ever had. I felt relieved to be paddling with them rather than with a pod of orca, another species that frequents these waters. It made me think about attempts to ban whaling, an issue on which many Australians hold firm views. I had always been a staunch opponent of commercial whaling, and this interaction galvanised my resolve to support efforts to stop it. These were intelligent, beautiful animals and deserved protection – an emotional and subjective position, but my opinion nonetheless.

The whales moved on after a few final sprays, leaving me alone to absorb this humbling experience. The animals of Alaska had welcomed me into their world (except perhaps the otters!) and shown me how truly amazing our world can be.

After a few hours of quiet exploration I made my way back to Kayakers Cove. When I arrived I went to work breaking down the kayak, to the bemused looks of the other paddlers, before packing it up for the long trip back to Sydney. I left a couple of FatPaddler.com stubby holders in the kitchen for future visitors, and walked down to the rocky ramp to wait for Matt.

When he arrived I stowed my kit on board and made my way into the warmth of the captain's wheelhouse. Inside were two tired-looking middle-aged Alaskan men dressed in hunting gear, chatting away and joking with each other about their adventures. I introduced myself and gave them a brief run-down of my trip before listening to their stories of their recent hunt.

It seemed these two gents regularly set out on multi-day hunts together, and had come down from Anchorage to get out into the wilderness. They'd been goat hunting on the mountains behind Kayakers Cove and had spent almost a week climbing through the snow and ice, tracking the goats and avoiding the bears. After all their efforts, they had come away without a kill but with a fair dose of exhaustion. They didn't seem to mind, since they'd had a great time.

I've never been a hunter and classify myself as an animal lover, so I never feel easy around discussions about guns and shooting game. However, these blokes would have only taken enough to fill their freezers back home (they'd have to carry their game back down the mountain), so I was relaxed hearing their anecdotes. I wasn't comfortable with the big hunting rifles on the boat, but Alaska is full of large carnivorous animals, so I could see why they were necessary. More important to me was the life and vitality of these two older men, fed by regular excursions into the wild.

When we ended our boat trip in Seward, I let the two hunters leave first. Once they were out of earshot, Matt asked me how old I thought they were. I'd thought mid to late fifties, maybe even early sixties, but Matt smiled and shook his head. They were both 75! This staggering feat of fitness for two elderly gents brought home to me a clear message – keep active throughout your life, and you'll stay fitter, healthier and happier for far longer. These men were perfect examples of where I could be if I managed to keep up an active lifestyle – a far rosier future than fat, crippled and stuck in front of the television.

With those thoughts swirling through my mind I went to unpack my gear, but Matt stopped me and offered to let me rest, shower and freshen up on his floating home, a 75-foot ocean trawler named *Cathy G*. He would have to take off for another job, but was happy to hand me the keys to his home after knowing me for a matter of days. It was another example of the great hospitality I encountered, and I gladly took up the offer. After a few days living in the wilderness, a shower was absolute bliss.

When Heidi arrived to take me to the train station, I told her a few stories from my travels and we had a good laugh before I thanked her and bade her goodbye. Then I was back on the train to Anchorage, where I had a few hours to stare out the window at glaciers and think about my adventure in the wilds of Alaska.

My thoughts centred on the way our lives change direction. I'd loved the outdoors as a child, regularly hiking in my local national park as a teenager. I'd played competitive sport from the time I was ten. I'd been enthralled by nature and the beauty of Australia's bush and deserts. Yet somewhere along the line I'd decided that pubs and nightclubs were more fun than days spent in the bush or on the water, and I'd missed nearly two decades of outdoor pursuits. I don't know what triggered this self-destructive behaviour, but being in the wilderness again showed me that happiness wasn't to be found in a bar or at a cash register. Real happiness was cheap, readily available and could be found all over the world. I just needed to get back outside to embrace it.

On that train journey I vowed that I would never again sacrifice real happiness for an artificial substitute. I would return to the outdoors every week to recharge, and I would share it with my family. I would make sure that my kids experienced camping, paddling, sailing and hiking, and then perhaps they would develop their own passion for the natural world.

It had taken something close to physical and mental destruction to push me down the path to real recovery. Not just physical recovery, but deep emotional and spiritual recovery. It had taken that level of desperation to get me back outdoors and into the real world again, and to reconnect with my own planet. It felt invigorating, like a rebirth, a renewal of purpose.

I watched my final Alaskan sunset as the train passed a tiny town across the Cook Inlet called Hope. That was exactly what this journey had given me. Hope for a longer life, more time with my kids, and true happiness.

Paddling past icebergs,
Bear Glacier Lake, Alaska.

Chapter 15
Final preparations

I RETURNED TO SYDNEY A NEW MAN. EXCITED, energetic and enthused about what lay ahead. However, my return home was marred by a frosty reception from my wife. She was not at all happy about my Alaskan adventure. My time away had meant she'd had to look after the kids alone for longer, and that I'd also spent money that could have been put towards a family holiday, all for what seemed to her to be a childish desire to go camping.

'I need to keep motivating myself Bec, or else I'm never going to get better,' I said, trying to reason with her. 'The girls deserve to have a father and I'm not going to be any use to them if I die of a heart attack at 40.'

'What, and risking your life in Alaska is a responsible way to be a father? You're just making excuses for spending the money.'

'C'mon Bec, that's not true and you know it. My work trip got me to the US, it was only a couple of hundred dollars to travel to Alaska, and I camped and stayed in hostels. We couldn't have had a weekend away on the coast for that money. And you know that I need the paddling to get well.'

To make matters worse, I was now training more often and for longer periods of time for the Hawkesbury Classic, a mere two months away. Between all the paddling and my trip abroad, Rebecca had to take on far more of the child care than before, and she resented it. Just when I really needed her support to keep training, it was quickly waning. It was driving a real wedge between us.

I had to rethink my position. Alaska had stirred a desire within me to return to the outdoors, to find happiness through nature. But Alaska hadn't checked with my wife and she was crucial to my happiness. I would have to find some middle ground, because I wasn't prepared to lose out on either – I needed my wife and family, but I needed to look after myself as well.

This is a problem common to so many marriages. You pledge to spend the rest of your life together, move in, have kids, and then give up all the parts of yourself that made you who you are.

Sometimes I'd bring this point up when the tension boiled over.

'You know Bec, remember when we met and I used to play rugby, DJ'd at parties and collected 70s furniture. I've given all of it up, everything that made me who I was. You can't expect me not to have any interests.'

'Oh, you think it's just you that's given things up?' she'd reply. 'What have I got now? I don't go out anymore, I have to look after the kids, and most of my friends have moved away from Sydney. We hardly have any family here to help and I have to do everything myself.'

The growth of my blog FatPaddler.com added more stress. It had gone from a couple of hundred visitors in its first month in April, to three-and-a-half thousand by September. My little journal was gaining attention from all over the world, as people embraced my efforts to become physically active as an inspiration for their own struggles. Emails asking for advice starting dribbling in, then built to a regular weekly stream. Story writing, photo processing, email responses and general site maintenance were becoming a serious daily overhead so I worked on the blog once the rest of my household had gone to sleep. The time I was now spending on paddling-related activities was not going unnoticed, and relations continued to cool in my household.

Despite the stresses, I had to keep going with the Hawkesbury Classic. I started to put in 20- and 25-km paddles through Sydney's national parks. This was helped by my acquisition of another kayak, a five-and-half-metre long second hand sea kayak from Canada. This boat was sleeker, faster and more comfortable than my first boat and would be perfect to take me the distance come the end of October.

I also made a new discovery. My local kayak shop down at The Spit in Sydney stocked a small supply of strange handmade wooden paddles that looked like flat sticks. They were based on the traditional paddles used by the Inuit, the indigenous peoples of the Arctic who invented the kayak. I decided to take one out for a test paddle.

From the first time I used one I fell in love. The craftsmanship was beautiful, the shape fitted perfectly in the hand, the stick seemed to sing as it passed through the water and, most importantly, it reduced the strain on my shoulders and arms enormously. This paddle worked almost as well as the paddles I'd been using, but with a fraction of the effort.

I did more research on the paddles, which were commonly referred to as Greenland paddles, or GPs for short. They were having quite a renaissance in the northern hemisphere, particularly among paddlers who travelled long distances and needed to conserve strength and energy. Furthermore, they were great for people with shoulder injuries, for breast cancer survivors who had had mastectomies, or for anyone who needed a paddle that was easier on their body. With my combined injury count, this style of paddle was perfect.

Over the next few weeks I acquired two of these paddles. The first was the paddle I'd tested at The Spit, and the second was custom made for me by Tom, a great bloke on the NSW Central Coast. The paddle Tom carved for me was stunning – incredibly light, long in the blade, and finished to perfection. After testing it, I had no doubt that this was going to be my weapon of choice for the Hawkesbury Classic.

The next item to organise was my landcrew. This would involve a land-based support team who would help get me on the water, and then keep me fed and watered throughout the long paddle. I wanted to make sure I had a crack team of seasoned professionals to look after me. But since I didn't know any, I had to make do with some of my friends.

The first person I picked was an old mate of mine, Burnsie. As team captain, he had overall responsibility for my welfare and would make sure everything was prepared and ready. He also happened to be an ex-Navy man who'd spent eleven years on ships cooking meals for sailors – the perfect background for someone on my crew! With him on board we talked at length about pre-race carb loading, during race carb maintenance and other boring parts of race preparation. We also talked about the flavours I wanted, how much chocolate I needed packed, and what sort of coffee I preferred, which I deemed far more important.

The second crewman was Grumm, a neighbour. Despite being both English and a supporter of the rubbish football team Sunderland, he was a half decent fella who could drive my car and would be handy for carrying heavy things like boats. His cutting Pommy wit and tendency to moan and complain made him perfect as entertainment for the team, and I willing accepted him into the fold.

The third and last member had a crucial role to play – combat systems officer. This person's role was to run cameras, video, computers and social media to ensure a steady flow of content could be streamed from the event to friends, family and fans of FatPaddler.com. To meet these criteria, the team was joined by the CEO of a technology company based in Brisbane, a New Zealander known to the team as Dazza. His Kiwi wit was even drier than Grumm's and together they made a formidable comedy duo.

With the three team members signed up, I could concentrate on training. I still had not paddled more than 25 km in a single sitting and was starting to worry about the task ahead. Since I'd started paddling I'd put in a good 600 km in the water, but a long distance training paddle still eluded me. I had also never paddled at night, nor paddled on the Hawkesbury River.

Around this time a paddler named Ned who lived in the country wrote to me about my website and his experiences on Hawkesbury Classics. He'd done the race a few times before as a young man, but not for the past ten years or more, and was interested in having another go. He was also travelling to within a few hundred kilometres of me, so we agreed to meet halfway for an evening paddle. We decided on the Wyong River, about an hour's drive north of Sydney.

Ned was waiting with his orange beast of a sea kayak, fittingly named *The Kraken*. His boat was big, plastic and roomy, and looked like it could carry an expedition for a year. It paddled exceptionally well and I could see why he loved the big tug.

Ned and I hit it off immediately, chatting casually to each other like old friends as we paddled. We continued on for hours after dark, enjoying the beauty of paddling under the stars. By the end of the night, we had decided to paddle the Classic together in our respective boats to keep each other company.

The next item I had to check off was to chalk up a decent distance, ideally on the Hawkesbury River. Two weeks out from the event, I launched my kayak from the Brooklyn boat ramp, the designated finish line for the Classic, and commenced upstream under a blazing sun. With a GPS unit strapped on the front deck, I could monitor both the distance and the speed I was making to estimate my likely progress on race day.

I really struggled on this training paddle, pushing myself up the river but never seeming to make real progress. After about 10 km I put the paddle down and reached for some water, admiring the beautiful red cliffs around the river valley reflecting the sunshine down onto the water. As I glanced down at the GPS I noticed I was making a steady 3 kilometres an hour, which was odd since I wasn't paddling. When I looked up I realised I was actually going backwards!

The Hawkesbury River is tidal, which means the water flows with the tide. One of the real pain points of the Hawkesbury Classic is that, due to the length of the race, paddlers are likely to face one, if not two incoming tides. Looking at my GPS I could see now just how much impact this would have, since I'd have to fight hard against a current moving at three kilometres an hour or more. I pushed off hard against the current to continue up the river.

I was shocked at the impact of the tide. I was straining hard to paddle and could barely clock up 4 kilometres an hour on the GPS. At this rate I wouldn't be able to finish the Classic inside the time limit of 20 hours. I pushed harder but that just exhausted me without increasing my speed. Two hours later I was still paddling hard, having barely added another 7 km to my tally. This was ridiculous. How the hell would I cope with the Classic?

I turned around and then got to enjoy having the current with me. Paddling at a steady pace I was now averaging 11 to 12 kilometres an hour, and was flying back down the river. This was more like it! The countryside seemed even prettier now that I wasn't straining so hard. I really enjoyed the final burn back.

Then, out of nowhere, the weather changed. I faced a hard-blowing southerly headwind, which slowed me down and made the paddle a hard struggle again. With 5 km to go, enormous black thunderclouds rolled in over the sky and I started to worry about the likelihood of a massive storm hitting me. With only a kilometre to go, lightning flashed above the hills around me, and huge raindrops started to come down. As I pulled into the boat ramp, the rain became a torrential downpour, with thunder and lightning booming all around me. By the time I was packed up and in the shelter of the car, a full-blown tropical storm was smashing Sydney, taking out powerlines and most of the northern suburbs' power supply for the rest of the day.

The final GPS reading was 35 km, a third of the race I'd be undertaking thirteen days later. I was sore and exhausted, but a little more confident. I was concerned about weather changes, though, so started to rethink the clothing, food and emergency equipment in case a similar storm hit in the dark during the race.

The big bloody paddle

Chapter 16
A bloody big paddle

I WOKE EARLY ON RACE DAY. I'D TRIED TO GET A GOOD night's sleep but was barely able to due to the excitement, spending much of the night lying in the dark running through all my preparations. By 6 a.m. I was up and about, sorting through clothes and equipment one last time to make sure I hadn't forgotten anything.

Dazza had flown in from Brisbane the day before and stayed at my home overnight, so we had breakfast with my family just before Grumm and Burnsie arrived. Then the boys went to work checking and re-checking my kit, trying to keep me calm. Dazza was all over the electronic stream, posting photos and live commentary across the web to friends and fans across the world. Feedback was coming in with people wishing me luck and a safe journey, as well as a flood of last-minute donations. I'd already raised thousands of dollars largely via the internet and felt immensely grateful to the global paddling community for getting behind me with so much support and so many generous donations.

I gave final kisses to Rebecca and my little girls before all four blokes in Team Fat Paddler T-shirts piled into the car for the long trip to Windsor in Sydney's north-west where the race was to start. The lads were all ripping into me by now, giving me plenty of grief about being the fattest bloke on the river that night, and asking whether the caterers had been warned I was coming.

When we arrived the place was abuzz with paddle folk. Hundreds of cars were arriving, all carrying various boats to take part in the race. The event usually involves over 600 paddlers, so the number of kayaks being prepared for the event was staggering. More disturbingly, my kayak looked like a slow tub in comparison with the sleek speed machines that made up the bulk of the boats. I had thought it was more of a social charity event, but it became clear that this was a super competitive event with some very serious athletes.

We found a good spot to set up and unload the boat. As the lads prepared my kit, Ned arrived with his groundcrew – his wife Megan, and her best friend Jody. They joined us and immediately the girls hit it off with my lads, cracking jokes at both Ned's and my expense. With five troublemakers on landcrew duties, the tone for the night was set. They were going to be loud and they were going to have fun. I just hoped they were also going to look after their paddlers.

Ned and I registered and had our boats checked by the race officials before settling down for a last meal. Burnsie had made an incredible pasta salad and Ned and I both tucked into a decent feed, loading up on as many carbs as we could. The meal was great, but Ned was quiet and subdued. I asked if he was okay and he admitted he was a chronic migraine sufferer and that one had started to build. He was desperate to lose it before the race started.

With the race just an hour away, the race organisers held their race briefing with all the competitors and landcrew. The event had raised over $250,000 for leukaemia research, a terrific fundraising success. The weather was looking to be good – a warm sunny afternoon with a little cloud cover at night. All the race checkpoints were set up and staffed, and all that was left to do was to have a few stretches and prepare to hit the water.

My stomach was churning with nervous energy. Less than a year earlier I'd been grossly unfit, smoking, drinking, morbidly obese and suffering multiple health problems. Had I done enough preparation for this endurance event? Would my injuries hold up to spending nearly a day in the kayak? Was I mentally prepared for the pain and exhaustion?

I had many doubts about my ability but the time had come. All I could do was follow my lads down to the river, watch as they slid my boat into the water, and climb aboard. Then I let my boat drift out into the mass of other starters preparing for the first starting wave, and waited for Ned to catch up in *The Kraken*.

The race is split up into 70 classes, determined by boat type, age and sex of the participants. The first wave is a non-competitive class called 'Brooklyn or Bust', designed for those who just want to finish. All manner of boats line up for this class, from the slowest short wide river boats to the fastest of ocean skis. Two of the boats were made of aluminium, and had been used recently for an Antarctic crossing, their enormous tank-like structures looking like they'd be incapable of anything more than a few knots.

Ned pulled up alongside me and we waved to our landcrew on the bank. Then, with a flourish, the race starter fired his pistol and we were away, bunched up in a mass of boats all trying to forge into the clear waters ahead of the pack. Ned and I were determined to take the start slowly and not burn up too much energy early in the race, but with everyone powering away it was hard not to up the tempo. We stepped up the rating a little and soon a few of the really slow boats fell behind us, as all the race starters began to spread a little across the river.

There was no time for nerves. It very much felt like a race. I couldn't quite fathom the fact I'd still be doing this in twelve hours, and instead enjoyed the competitiveness on the water. Ned was struggling with his migraine, and despite trying to keep a smile on his face, I could see the pain building up behind his eyes. I tried to keep his spirits up

A night training paddle on the Wyong river.

▲ Team Fat Paddler on the morning of the 2009 Hawkesbury Classic
(from left to right: Darryl King, Sean, Paul Grummett, Brett Burns).

▲ Ned tries to smile for the camera despite a crippling migraine.

▲ The beginnings of the bloody big paddle.

▲ The last moments of light before the long paddle through the night.

▲ Burnsie's chicken noodle soup was a godsend at the 35 km mark.

▲ Coming in hard for the big finish of the 2009 Hawkesbury Classic!

▲ Training on Sydney Harbour at sunrise.

▲ The Fat Paddler and his girls.

Sean with his Greenland paddle.

▲ Sydney – the world's most beautiful paddling backdrop?

The pink dawn at Mosman, Sydney. A great way to start any day.

with a few jokes directed at other competitors, and we continued down the river.

Fifteen minutes after our start the next wave left the starting line. A different class would start every fifteen minutes until six o'clock in the evening, when the uber fast boats were unleashed. For now, we were still at the head of the race and the banter between paddlers on the water was fun and relaxed. One of the boats nearby had a stereo onboard and its young paddler was piping a calypso version of 'Row Row Row Your Boat' through it across the water, to much laughter from the rest of us.

It wasn't long until the next wave caught us. It was still a 'Brooklyn or Bust' class, but it was the doubles. Double kayaks are longer and have more power than single craft, and these paddlers flew past us on the water. Occasionally, someone would ask me about my weird Greenland paddle, or crack jokes about how I was going to do it tough if I continued to paddle with a stick. A few paddlers even recognised me as the Fat Paddler and called out my name as they went past.

The river kept winding as we continued the race, and after 12 km we came across the first checkpoint, a jetty in the Cattai National Park. As we paddled up to it, I could see our landcrew crowding in on deck yelling out, 'Paddle faster Fatty!' as I approached them. Ned managed a weak laugh through his building migraine, and after a very quick stop for water, we continued down the river.

The day was still hot as we made our way into a wilder part of the river. Huge sandstone cliffs and pristine bushland lined the riverbanks, and I started to enjoy the race. We'd done 15 km and I felt great, cruising along and enjoying the view of the bush. Ned's condition, on the other hand, was rapidly declining as his migraine turned to blinding pain. He was silent, paddling much of the time with his eyes closed, and I was worried about his ability to continue. Still, as dusk started to fall, we continued paddling, with me slowing down a little to make sure I stayed with him. He protested that I should leave him and go, that he didn't want to slow me down, but I just shrugged off his suggestion. No matter how long it took, we'd get to the major checkpoint at the 30 km mark together, and that was a promise.

Darkness was almost upon us and the glow of Cyalumes, attached to all the competitors' boats were becoming the major feature on the water. Ned was in serious distress. He vomited across the deck of his kayak and I doubted his ability to go on, but he managed to keep putting in the paddle strokes as we slowly continued down the river.

When darkness closed in we still had several kilometres to go. I concentrated on talking to Ned and trying to keep his spirits up long enough to bring him in. I'd only ever had one or two migraines in my life and knew that they can be so severe as to be crippling. He was quietly concentrating on each paddle stroke, barely aware of what was going on around him, and I stayed close in case he collapsed. The kilometres went past and other paddlers flew by until finally, in the distance, I could make out the flashing lights of a ferry crossing. The checkpoint was just past the crossing so I talked up the fact it was nearly over and that we would be able to have a rest soon. Somehow Ned managed to grin in the darkness and push on.

When we arrived at the ferry crossing we paused to wait for the ferry to dock on the bank, before paddling on past and around a bend in the river. Then, with 30 km behind us, the bright lights of the Sackville major checkpoint appeared and we coasted our boats into the packed beach.

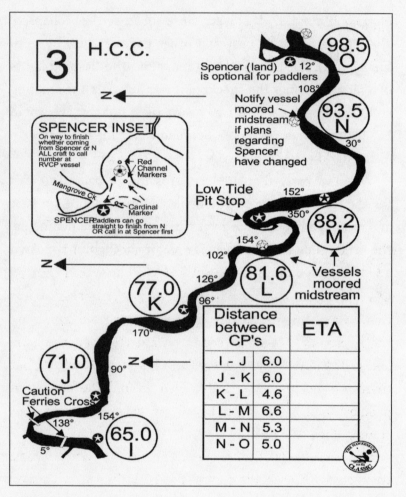

3 H.C.C.

SPENCER INSET
On way to finish
whether coming
from Spencer or N
ALL craft to call
number at
RVCP vessel

← Red
Channel
Markers

Mangrove Ck

← Cardinal
Marker

SPENCER paddlers can go
straight to finish from N
OR call in at Spencer first

Spencer (land) 12° is optional for paddlers
108°

Notify vessel
moored
midstream
if plans
regarding
Spencer
have changed

Low Tide
Pit Stop

152°

350°

154°

102°

126°

96°

170°

90°

138°

154°

5°

Caution
Ferries Cross

Vessels
moored
midstream

98.5 O

93.5 N
30°

88.2 M

81.6 L

77.0 K

71.0 J

65.0 I

Distance between CP's		ETA
I - J	6.0	
J - K	6.0	
K - L	4.6	
L - M	6.6	
M - N	5.3	
N - O	5.0	

Stage map 3 for the Hawkesbury Classic, Wisemans Ferry
to Spencer

Chapter 17
Hell's tide

NED AND I FOUGHT OUR WAY THROUGH THE CROWD of boats on the beach until we hit land. I climbed out of my kayak before helping Ned get out of his, then turned to look for our landcrew among the crowds on the riverbank. I couldn't see them anywhere on the bank and called out, 'Team Fat Paddler! Team Fat Paddler!', but there was no response. I stumbled around the masses of paddlers and crews until I saw my lads and Ned's girls coming down the hill.

They quickly set up some chairs for us and Burnsie went to work with his camp stove, heating up a chicken and pasta soup he'd made fresh the night before. Dazza snapped a few photos before giving my shoulders a quick massage, while Megan and Jody led Ned over to the medical tent for evaluation. Burnsie handed me a hot bowl of soup and some buttered white bread which I attacked with a hunger built during hours of hard paddling. I hoped Ned was all right and took stock of my own condition.

The 30 km had been hard and I felt a little stiffness in my shoulders and a bit of a dull ache in my pelvis. But I couldn't wait to attack the next 30 km. Whether the feeling was due to adrenaline or endorphins, I felt an incredible natural high and was itching to keep going. I wanted to wait for news on Ned, however, so I allowed myself a half-hour break as the lads restocked the boat and handed me some thermal clothes to get into for the cold night's paddling ahead.

When Megan returned, the news was bad. Ned was far too sick to continue and had to withdraw from the race. The lads got Ned's boat and gear back to their car and, with a final handshake, I said goodbye as he was led away. Grumm and Dazza helped me back into my kayak and, with a final few words of encouragement, 'Paddle faster next time you fat bastard!', they pushed me out into the darkness.

I was fired up to keep going but saddened by the loss of Ned. Not only was I worried about him, I'd planned on leaning on his experience to keep me going when things got tough. Now I was pushing off down the Hawkesbury in the dark, feeling very much alone.

Quite a few had passed me on the first leg, many giving me a hard time about my Greenland paddle, but I now found myself catching a few of them up. Like any endurance race, there are those that go hard too early and burn out, and now I was paddling past a heap of them with my funny looking paddle. I tried not to be too smug, but it was hard not to be proud of my little wooden stick.

There were many others who were just cruising along, and I had a chat with a fair few as I was going past. The less competitive types were like me, ordinary people pushing their own limits and hoping just to finish. Among us, there was a strong sense of camaraderie. There were also lots of paddlers in tandem boats fighting, a phenomenon I'd heard about. People's limits of endurance are different, so paddlers need breaks at different times, annoying the partner who doesn't need to rest. Ned told me about a tandem experience he'd had where relations broke down so much, the friendship was permanently destroyed.

Paddling under the stars was beautiful. I could no longer see the surrounding hills or cliffs, but for an hour or so the stars and moon shone down from the sky while distant Cyalumes glowing on the horizon marked out the position of other paddlers on the water. I took a deep breath of the chilled night air and concentrated on remembering the peaceful swish of my paddle through the quiet countryside of Australia. It was hard to believe I was actually doing this.

After an hour the sky started to cloud over, covering the stars and moon making the landscape darker. It was pitch black and I could barely see where the water ended and the banks begun, and was totally dependent on following the Cyalumes spread out in front of me. I was now very much paddling by feel and by GPS, which showed me a map of the river and my position on it.

Then everything just got harder. I didn't understand at first what was happening, as my boat seemed to slow down and the passing checkpoints seemed to take forever to reach. My pelvis hurt a little but my shoulders were really aching. My paddle felt heavier and slower as it passed through the water. It was as if my paddling engine was slowing running to a halt.

I pulled out a muesli bar and shoved it into my mouth, chewing quickly before washing it down with a sports drink. Perhaps I simply needed more food and water, and I'd perk up. But as I paddled on down the river, things didn't improve. My speed slowed further and the paddling became more difficult. Then I thought to check the tide charts, and I realised what had happened. I was paddling against an incoming tide, which I'd have to fight for the next few hours.

This was tough news. A quick check of the GPS showed I'd done about 40 km, leaving another 70 km to go. I'd never paddled this far before and I was starting to hurt and feel really tired. The bloody tide was dragging at my boat with every stroke and my pace slowed to half that of the first leg as every muscle in my back, arms and shoulders ached. I had to do something to take my mind off the remaining distance, something to take my mind of the pain.

I thought about the book *Crossing the Ditch* I'd read recently. The two paddlers, Justin and Jonesy, had spent over 60 days on the Tasman Sea, and here I was whimpering about a few hours' paddling. Those guys had paddled against ocean currents, and I was whinging about a little river tide. Clearly I'd be able to keep going if I had to, I just needed to harden up and stop being such a princess.

Only 20-odd km away was another major checkpoint and a hot meal. If I concentrated on that distance it would be far easier to cope with and, at my current pace, only about four hours away. Despite my building pain it was a beautiful night and there were other paddlers to talk to. I tried not to think about the problems.

The hours went by and my fatigue grew harder to ignore. The tide was agony to fight. Every stroke felt like pulling my paddle through honey. I tried to concentrate on this part of the race but the thought of having to paddle another 50 or 60 km nagged at the back of my mind. Was it even possible considering the pain I was in? Had I been stupid to take on an event of such magnitude so soon? Perhaps with my injuries I was mad to have entered this race at all.

The doubts continued to rage as I put the paddle blades in the water, heading north up the river. Midnight turned into the early hours of the morning. I turned a bend in the river and far off in the distance I could see the flashing lights of Wisemans Ferry, the 65 km mark in the race.

This section is famous for breaking the hearts of paddlers. The second major checkpoint can be seen for many kilometres before paddlers reach it, so that against the tide it can take an hour or more to get to. I was in agony – my pelvis throbbing, my shoulders heaving, and my back aching – but I had another few hundred paddle strokes to reach it. At last, with a relieved sigh, I pulled into the carpeted boat ramp into the waiting hands of Dazza, Grumm and Burnsie.

The boys helped lift me out of the boat. My legs were like jelly but I was relieved to have made it this far. I had a pressing need to get to the men's room first and the boys pointed me in the right direction before washing out the kayak and restocking it. The toilets seemed to be miles away. By the time I reached them, I was shivering. The temperature was close to 3 degrees.

When I returned to the boys I was seriously cold, and they went to work rugging me up. Burnsie put another hot bowl of soup into my hands and I slurped it down, needing its sustenance badly and happy to be full of something hot. Then Burnsie pulled out some freshly ground coffee and went to work making a big strong, bitter pot of it.

At this point I made a dire tactical error. I was cold, tired, and not thinking straight, and demanded more and more coffee to help perk me up. After three big mugs of the strong dark stuff, my kidneys went into overdrive and I found myself busting for the toilet again. After making the trek to the toilet block and back, I discovered I needed to go again! This time I ducked down to the river bank to relieve myself, but after returning to our little camp and climbing into my warm thermals, I needed to go yet again! If this was any indication of what was to come, I was going to be in trouble, because there just aren't that many places after Wisemans Ferry where you can pull over. I had packed a hospital urine bottle as a 'bailer', but very much hoped I wouldn't need it. Now I was quietly relieved it was there!

The boys led me back down to the boat and helped me climb back in. The stop had taken far longer than planned, but I felt much better. I had close to 50 km to go, which seemed an enormous distance. But I'd passed the halfway mark and soon the tide would be in my favour. Feeling a little happier, I pushed off into the darkness for the final leg.

Team Fat Paddler won the 2009 Landcrew award,
otherwise known as 'the teabag'

Chapter 18
Running on empty

THE HAWKESBURY RIVER DOES A BIG WIDE LOOP around Sydney. It starts far out west of the metropolis and meanders north-east for over 60 km before turning for the south-east run back to the ocean. Wisemans Ferry is at the apex of this journey, ending the northerly route and starting the southerly track back towards Sydney and the sea.

As I left Wisemans Ferry, two things happened. Firstly, unbelievably, I needed the toilet again. The 'bailer' got its first use for the night and I was not even 200 metres from my last nature stop! Secondly, a thick fog rolled in over the river, taking visibility to zero. This was troubling because I'd been navigating largely by following other paddlers' Cyalumes. That was now out of the question. I also used green or red channel markers which shone in the dark like beacons, but this could be dangerous, as I was about to find out.

I paddled through the fog, heading towards a green channel marker in the hazy distance. I checked with my GPS and it was telling me that I'd missed the turn south, and that I was heading for the far bank of the river. This made no sense at all until I realised the green 'channel marker' I'd been drawn to was some sort of light on land, and I was on a collision course with the opposite bank.

I cursed and vowed never to doubt the GPS again, as I turned back to where it said I should be going. Sure enough, I found the turn where it said it would be and paddled through the final ferry crossing before turning into the dark river valley beyond. I was safely out of Wisemans and on my way on the long, dark route to the next major stop 35 km away.

Everything was hurting now. My pelvic pain had reached new levels of agony. Time to take a few painkillers. I swallowed a couple of paracetamol tablets and hoped they'd act fast. My hands were blistering so I pulled on paddling gloves. My shoulders and arms were getting worse as the lactic acid built up and each paddle stroke became more difficult. My hips were developing pressure sores from the side of the kayak, with each stroke rubbing the sores and making them worse.

But at least every kilometre I paddled was one I could put behind me. Despite the difficult task ahead, I knew that I'd already achieved a great distance and had no intention of stopping. I continued into the night, pushing through the pain and stopping only to use the bailer every fifteen minutes or so, silently cursing the earlier cups of coffee.

I was alone with my thoughts battling the pain that seemed to be coming from every part of my body. I thought about my family, and how they had given me the will to live. I thought about my wife during my dark days in hospital, who had come in religiously to see me despite having to work and even though she was carrying our baby. I thought about the excruciating pain I'd been in for months when my pelvis was broken. Nothing I was feeling now could compare with that level of intense, never-ending agony. As I forced myself to think about these things, the sky slowly lightened and the sun came up over the hills.

For the first time in many hours I could see the landscape around me. The river was now wide, with huge sandstone cliffs in the surrounding hills reflecting the red and orange of the sunrise. Green mangroves lined the river as far as the eye could see, and in the water huge basketball-like jellyfish floated by. The scene was absolutely stunning, but I was completely exhausted and in pain. I allowed myself to pull over for a couple of minutes, where I had a quick whimpering cry, before pulling back out into the river.

My paddling was now weak. I could barely pull the blade through the water and my pace slowed. I wondered if the tide was changing but when I checked my charts I found it wasn't due to turn against me for another few hours. I was completely spent, sore, tired, and desperately wanted the whole thing to end.

Meanwhile, my landcrew had been camping out at Spencer, the last major stop 15 km before the finish line. The stop was often skipped by paddlers because pulling into it added 4 extra kilometres to the paddle, but I'd figured I was going to need it to restock. The crew could track my pace on the race leaderboard as I checked into each checkpoint spaced several kilometres apart throughout the course. My progress since leaving Wisemans Ferry had been agonisingly slow and they had been waiting for hours, growing increasingly worried.

When I reached the last checkpoint before Spencer I had to choose whether to pull in or continue to the end and shave off the 4 km. In my poor physical and mental state I should have gone in for a quick break, especially as I'd just run out of water. But the thought of those extra kilometres was too much to bear, and I told the checkpoint that I would go on to the finish. Their job was to relay the information onto my landcrew at Spencer so they could drive the last hour to the finish line.

Unfortunately, the message got lost along the way. It wasn't until some time later that the lads discovered that far from of being lost, I was racing past checkpoints further downstream at almost twice my previous speed. They hurried to the Brooklyn Bridge finish line, calling my wife on the way to advise her I was only a few hours away, and wondering how I'd picked up so much speed.

On the water I was starting to charge. There's something in me that loves a final sprint, and my old competitive spirit had taken over. With 15 km to go I'd picked up my pace to almost twice what it had been throughout the night, powering into the wind while checking out the other competitors on the same stretch of water. If paddlers looked to be gaining on me, or if I could see paddlers ahead, I'd add speed. I was still exhausted, in pain, and now also dehydrating, but with the end so close I no longer cared. It was time to finish this damn race, and I was going to do it hard.

Every now and then I'd collapse and pull over for half a minute's rest. My body simply refused to be pushed further and demanded that I stop. I'd suck in some big breaths and then as soon as I'd spy paddlers catching me up I'd be off again, pushing hard down the river towards the finish line.

When I passed the final checkpoint, almost eighteen hours had passed since the start of the race. My pelvis was screaming, my hands were blistered and my hips now streamed blood into the boat from the pressure sores. But I could see the finish line only a couple of kilometres away, and my pace picked up to full sprint, racing along the final stretch. My Greenland paddle sang as it whirred through the water. This was it, the final burst of energy before achieving the goal I'd set several months before.

I took a quick moment to think about my journey. The damage I'd done to myself would have killed me several times over had it not been for the miracle of modern medicine. I had smashed my body completely, and yet here I was about to achieve a significant athletic feat. I quietly thanked the doctors and nurses responsible for my recovery before setting my sights firmly on the finish line.

The Team Fat Paddler boys couldn't believe what they were seeing. They hadn't expected me to come in for at least another hour and here I was, powering towards the finish line. My speed over the last 15 km was so much faster than they expected that my wife hadn't even arrived, and was going to miss my finish. The boys dutifully filmed my approach as I came in to the boat ramp, where my name was called out and I was congratulated by the race caller while I coasted the final few metres to shore.

I was ecstatic. I'd managed to beat my demons and finish this gruelling race, not as a super-fit athlete, but as an everyday normal bloke. The months of training, the early morning starts in the cold, the gym work with Dirk the Smiling Assassin, and even the paddling in Alaska – everything had come together to help me push myself for eighteen hours through the night, earning the right to say 'Yes, I finished the Hawkesbury Canoe Classic.' It was bliss.

My wife arrived with a bag of McDonalds, a naughty but nice treat after the night's exertion. As I tucked into a cheese burger, someone asked me if I was going to do the race again the following year. I looked at them deadpan and replied, 'You must be stupid. I'm never, ever, *ever* doing this bloody race again!'

Sean and Gelo, chasing a kayak in the
2010 Hawkesbury Classic.

Chapter 19
What next?

I'VE ALWAYS BEEN A GOAL-ORIENTED PERSON SO finishing the Hawkesbury Canoe Classic left a void. Friends, colleagues and website fans asked 'What next?' but I had no answer. I had a fair bit of thinking to do about my personal goals, and those for the Fatpaddler.com website which was now entertaining over 6000 people a month.

I decided that I'd like to learn to paddle out to sea, or at the very least along the coast, and that meant developing a new range of skills. It also meant I'd need to change my boat to something more suited to messy water, so I bought a shiny new red sea kayak specially designed for more technical paddling.

The first skill I wanted to learn was rolling, a difficult technique that involves falling upside down into water while strapped into your kayak, then using a series of movements to roll back upright again. This skill is particularly useful for self-rescues when in the dangerous environments of sea and coastal surf, so I took myself off to get a lesson with one of Sydney's top instructors.

I had to learn to steer my new kayak by shifting my body weight and using special strokes. I learnt to catch small waves and boat wake and was able to surf my boat across the harbour. I set out every week, and my confidence slowly built as I learned to paddle this very different kind of boat.

The website continued to develop as I posted more details of my paddling, and more beginners wrote to me each week asking for advice on how to start. I answered all the emails and helped people find the right boats to get them outdoors and help them build healthier lives. As I did this, the essence of FatPaddler.com became clear to me. I wanted the site to continue the three key objectives I'd had when I started – to get non-athletic people outdoors and exercising (whether they be old, fat, injured, disabled, or just plain lazy); to show people the fun to be had outdoors on the water; and to raise money and awareness for charity.

With that in mind, I entered 'Lifestart Kayak for Kids', a charity paddle on Sydney Harbour that raises money for children with developmental problems. I talked a bunch of friends into doing it with me, and together we trained and raised funds for the 18-km social paddle, coming together on the water as Team Fat Paddler.

Before that event, I entered an ocean paddle race from the Harbour Bridge to Manly – the Bridge to Beach.

With paddler mate Tim Kennings, we took to the ocean ski race in our slow sea kayaks and with Greenland paddles. On a day that brought forth the worst weather conditions in the history of the race, we bounced our sea kayaks through 2-metre ocean swells and gale-force headwinds to the finish at Manly Beach, to the cheers of the crowds lining the shore.

The Kayak for Kids event a few weeks later was a huge success, with our team raising thousands of dollars for Lifestart, as well as providing plenty of laughs on the water as we took to other competitors with water guns. The Team Fat Paddler name was forging a reputation at events for fun and hard work on the fundraising stakes, increasing the profile of the website with local and international paddlers.

As more paddlers became aware of the site and my story, I started receiving emails from people with similar stories. My approach to recovery and living was resonating with far more people than I'd anticipated and most of the feedback was positive. Often I was asked for advice on how to start paddling and whether or not it was possible for people with various ailments. I'd reply to each email with as much relevant information as I could find, happy to be able to respond to so many different people.

Eventually the Fat Paddler brand gained the attention of the Boating Industry Association in Sydney, a body which caters to the bigger motor boats and yachts on Australia's waterways. They asked if I'd be interested in speaking about paddling at the Sydney International Boat Show. I was flattered to be asked to represent my sport and readily accepted the opportunity to speak on the same stage as Aussie adventurers Jessica Watson, Don McIntyre and two of my biggest inspirations, James and Jonesy of *Crossing the Ditch* fame. When I met my paddling idols I was as giddy as a schoolgirl on her first date. Frankly, I was an embarrassment!

Shortly after the boat show an event called Paddle for Pete was held to raise money for a surf lifesaver who had injured his spine in a freakish accident. On a cold, wet and windy morning hundreds of local paddlers on kayaks, skis, stand up paddle boards, surf boats and other paddle craft came together for a few laps around Sydney's Pittwater. The event raised tens of thousands of dollars to help Pete's family cope with his medical bills. It was a terrific example of local and paddler community spirit.

In October, despite all promises to the contrary, I lined up again for the Hawkesbury Canoe Classic. I was determined to put some fun back into the event and had entered a 14-foot tandem canoe with a mate from work nicknamed Gelo. Together, we would attempt the gruelling race in the widest, slowest boat on the water, but we'd do it for a laugh so we could help raise more funds for leukaemia research. We were rejoined by Team Fat Paddler members Grumm and Burnsie from the previous year's Classic, and a great bloke called Sacha who'd paddled in the team for Kayak for Kids.

The day of my second Classic started out hot and sunny but as it day drew closer to the race kick-off, dark storm clouds rolled across New South Wales and Sydney. Lightning broke out across the hills surrounding the start line and paddlers faced the daunting thought of having to paddle through an electrical storm.

Gelo and I started the race at 4.15 p.m. into a headwind which tired most of the paddlers, but with our onboard stereo cranking out tunes, we patiently plodded along at our own pace laughing and shouting encouragement to the paddlers around us. By the time we reached the first major checkpoint most of the competitors were ahead of us but after a feed of lamb sausages, care of Burnsie, we set off for the second part in the driving rain and wind.

The leg to Wisemans was tough in our plastic bathtub, especially as the rain continued relentlessly for the entire journey. When we pulled in at Wisemans Ferry around 3 a.m., like many other paddlers that night we were exhausted. Burnsie outdid himself again, cooking us a Canadian breakfast of pancakes, bacon and maple syrup. With bellies full of warm food, we set off again into the night.

The final leg of the race was a disaster. Around 4 a.m. a full-blown storm hit the Hawkesbury River region bringing gale-force head winds and driving rain, whipping up the water into three- and four-foot waves which crashed over us in our little canoe. We spent over an hour with our heads down paddling hard into the storm in the dark, unable to see where we were going and twice being caught by 'strainers' – fallen trees stretched out into the river – which almost took our heads off.

By daylight, when the storm eased, we were exhausted, but determined to get to the finish line. A constant rain beat down on us and we had to bail out the canoe every fifteen minutes, and a tide change fought against our progress. But we kept the canoe paddles in the water and slowly made our way towards the finish.

The conditions at the end of the race were so bad that paddlers were coming out of their boats utterly spent. The race organisers decided that the conditions were too dangerous and shortened the race to Spencer, at the 98 km mark. Gelo and I kept paddling against the tide until we reached the checkpoint before Spencer, 93.5 km down the river, when an Emergency Services boat made its way to us and told us the rest of the race had been called off. Seventeen and a half hours after we started, Gelo and I were disappointed not to have finished, but proud that we'd taken our little boat so far under such terrible conditions.

The event went down as featuring the worst weather conditions for a decade, but for me it was probably the highlight of the paddles I'd done. Despite the difficulties we faced, we had an amazing adventure paddling through the storm and felt truly alive by the end of it. We'd also put a few thousand dollars into the charity kitty, a decent amount to help the fight against leukaemia.

When that final race finished and as I was tucking into a meat pie with sauce at the Spencer General Store some time later, someone again asked the inevitable question.

'So Fat Paddler, are you going to do the Hawkesbury Classic again next year?'

Between mouthfuls of pie my answer was short but clear. 'Bloody oath!'

You never know, maybe I might see you there.

A reason to live: Grace and Ella.

Epilogue

Throughout the last few years I've been surprised at how many people have connected with my journey. Thousands of people yearn for something to improve their lives, their health and their general wellbeing. Sport can be difficult for people who are in bad physical shape, and paddling holds a great attraction for those who can't get up and go for a run.

Scores of people have written to me saying they understand exactly what I've gone through trying to deal with injury, a battle with weight and general middle-age spread. Some are genuinely inspired to give paddling a go, and I try to give them the best guidance in terms of how to start, where to go, what boats to try and how to meet other people in similar circumstances.

My blogging details many of the mistakes I've made, things that I've learnt, and things that I wish I hadn't done. There are plenty of people who criticise me for my mistakes and I'm pleased that they take the time to write to me and tell me why they feel the way they do. I have never claimed to be a paddling expert and make mistakes all the time. I'm glad I do, because it shows I'm willing to push myself beyond my comfort zone. That doesn't mean that I don't take safety precautions. Safety is particularly important for water sports.

My many spells in hospital have taught me that the human body is an amazing thing. I've been close to the edge twice. Knowing the extent of the damage I've done to myself I'm amazed and thankful that I made it through. Modern medicine, the skill of doctors and surgeons and the care of nurses have managed to keep me alive despite catastrophic injury. I am forever indebted to them and the health system.

Of course not everything can be cured. My accidents have left me permanently in pain and there's nothing that can be done about that. Some days it reaches terrible levels and I get grumpy and difficult to be around. Other days it's manageable. Life goes on and I can either moan and groan or get on with it and look for the positives. When I meet others with worse injuries than mine it reminds me that there is always someone worse off and we should all be thankful for what we have.

Cancer in its many forms kills way too many people, and the research needed to beat it needs substantial funding, drawn largely from charitable pursuits. That is why events like the Hawkesbury Classic are so important – not so much as a race, but as a way for normal folks to achieve something special for themselves while raising much-needed research dollars.

As a parent, sicknesses that affect children are particularly distressing to me. Charities that support research, treatment and family support do crucial work and I would urge my readers to reach into their pockets and give a little when they come calling. Events like the Lifestart Kayak for Kids are not only important as fundraisers, they are also a lot of fun. Whether you are a paddler or not, there are worse ways to support children than getting out on the water.

As I watch my children grow up it amazes me how quickly they adapt to technology. My daughter at two years old could happily navigate my iPhone and play games. Older children I know spend masses of time on their games consoles. While I'm a strong advocate of technology and work in an innovative industry, it worries me that our children don't get outside more to explore and connect with their environment.

When I was growing up I hiked in the local conservation park, played rugby with my school and club, surfed on the weekends, went dingy sailing with my father, swam at the beach with my friends and went camping during school holidays. Being outdoors was an integral part of the Aussie way of life, and it is still important for the all-round development of our kids.

When I turned eighteen I spent far too much time in clubs and bars. Early mornings were reserved for sleep-ins and hangovers, and these replaced the early morning drives to the surf or weekends away camping. Our society has too big a reliance on our drinking culture to the detriment of personal growth. Despite loving a cold beer or rum, I believe alcohol has a lot to answer for. The high of being a little tipsy doesn't remotely compare to the high of seeing the sun rise over the Tasman Sea from my kayak. My paddling has radically cut down my drinking.

Giving up smoking was, quite seriously, one of the hardest things I've ever done in my life. Like many smokers, I had tried unsuccessfully several times to quit the horrid things. If your friends are trying to give up, give them as much encouragement as possible.

Paddling has brought me much closer to the environment. A morning on Sydney's Middle Harbour after a deluge means paddling through tonnes of rubbish and oil. I am forever fishing out cans and plastic bags. On a global level, we need to be more aware of the ocean gyres where toxic plastic waste gathers and breaks down, to be ingested by fish and passed into the food chain. We need to remember that humans are at the top of that food chain. The gyres are now so huge that finding a way to clean them up is no longer possible. The only viable action is to stop the millions of tonnes of rubbish from entering our waterways.

It is hard to put my finger on any one reason I love paddling so much. The exercise is good, the fresh air even better. Being outdoors and among nature is awesome as well. There is something magical about salty spray in your face and seeing a seal or stingray under your boat. The biggest bonus is the great people I meet. Every time I get out on the water I am greeted with a smile and a wave by other paddlers. All over the world, paddlers share a passion for the water, and the rate at which they connect on social media shows how strong the paddling phenomenon has become. I can travel anywhere in the world, check the internet and a day later be on the water paddling with someone who shares the passion.

Despite my paddling, over the past few years I haven't actually lost that much weight. I still paddle and hit the gym once or twice a week, but my inability to run does make it hard to slim down. Even so, my cardiovascular fitness is excellent and my blood pressure is low, now that I no longer smoke and only occasionally drink alcohol. On the rare occasions I go to the doctor, I get a top bill of health. This is a long way from where I was two years ago, and I owe it all to my paddling obsession. As my doctor says, 'You're an incredibly fit man, trapped inside a fat bloke.' There are worse things to be!

The Fat Paddler Sealed Section
Favourite recipes

Burnsie's chicken noodle soup

During my first Hawkesbury Classic I asked Team Fat Paddler chef extraordinaire Burnsie to make me something that had carbs, plenty of liquid and lots of flavour. He arrived on the day having made a huge vat of his own chicken noodle soup, which was so good that other team members started trying to pilfer it. When I came into Sackville after paddling my first 30 km, Burnsie handed me a bowl of the hot soup and a soft fluffy piece of bread spread liberally with butter. At that moment in time I thought it was the greatest food I'd ever tasted!

Ingredients

- 2 tablespoons olive oil
- ½ bunch celery
- 3 carrots
- 1 onion
- 1 whole fresh chicken

- 2 cobs of fresh corn
- 1 tablespoon fresh thyme
- salt and freshly ground pepper to taste (I like lots of pepper)
- 500 grams dry spaghetti

Method

1 Heat oil in a large soup pot. Dice celery, carrots and onion and take the corn kernels off the cob. Add vegetables and saute for 5 minutes then set aside.

2 Cut chicken into pieces (take off the drumsticks and cut in half, cut off the wings, cut remaining carcass into quarters), place the chicken in the pot and cook for 15 minutes to give a nice golden colour and to glaze the bottom of the pot. Add sauteed vegetables and cover with boiling water. Add fresh thyme, salt and pepper. Bring to the boil and then turn down to a slow simmer for 2 hours.

3 Break up spaghetti into 4–5-cm lengths and add. Check that there is enough liquid and add more if necessary (I add about 2 cups during this stage). After 2 hours remove chicken from the pot and take out the bones (the bones give loads of extra flavour during cooking).

4 Break the flesh into chunks and put back in the soup. Check seasoning and add salt and pepper to taste.

5 Before serving add some fresh thyme on top. Best served with fresh toasted bread smothered in butter!

Meat chips with chipotle

Nestled in a backstreet in East Sydney, just out of the main business district, is a little Mexican restaurant called Café Pacifico. The food is sensational and the atmosphere crazy, as the boss rings a bell throughout the night which means tequila shots for the staff and anyone having a birthday.

On one such night after ordering copious shots of tequila, the boss brought out a glass of his own personal stash of Habanero Tequila and a bowl of chipotle chillies. I immediately fell in love with the chipotle's hot smoky flavour and then tempered it with tequila hotter than the surface of the sun. The last thing I remember was lying on my back in a garden hallucinating about possums with saucer-sized eyes running around me. Crazy stuff that Habanero Tequila!

For the uninitiated, chipotles are red jalapenos that are dried and smoked, then rehydrated and steeped in a lightly spiced tomato-based sauce. Their smokiness makes them delicious.

Ingredients
- 5 chorizo sausages
- 220 grams chipotle in adobo sauce
- 2 tablespoons extra virgin olive oil

Method
1 Lightly dry cook the chorizo on the barbecue or in a pan, until lightly browned. Remove from heat and leave to cool for 15 minutes before slicing thinly.
2 In a bowl, roughly chop the chipotles in the adobo and set aside. Heat the olive oil in a pan and re-fry the chorizo slices lightly, before pouring in the chopped chipotles. Stir well and saute for 5 minutes.
3 With a slotted spoon, remove the chorizo 'meat chips' and place in a bowl. Serve immediately.

Chorizo with onion and parsley

I work in the Chinatown end of the Sydney business district. In among the backpacker hostels and cheap Asian eateries is a Spanish restaurant called Encasa. It is famous for great pizza and tapas that is steeped in copious amounts of oil and garlic. Their chorizo dish needs to be quickly washed down with cold citrusy sangria to avoid the garlic burning your lips, but its aftertaste makes it so worthwhile!

Ingredients
- 4 tablespoons of extra virgin olive oil
- 1 medium brown onion, roughly diced
- 4 cloves of garlic, halved and thinly sliced
- 5 chorizo sausages, sliced into 1-cm lengths
- 1 bunch of continental parsley, roughly chopped

Method
1 Heat the olive oil in a large pan or wok. Add the diced onion and garlic and stir for two minutes or until the onion is transparent. Turn the heat down and allow the onion to slowly saute and caramelise.
2 Add the chorizo and stir through. Allow to cook in the oil for several minutes before pouring the entire mixture into a clay pot. Stir through the chopped parsley and serve immediately.

Spaghetti puttanesca

There are many stories as to the origin of this salty Sicilian pasta dish. I like to think the following is true.

The prostitutes of a small Sicilian town wanted to find a way to lure married men away from their wives and into the bordellos. To do so they came up with a flavoursome, salty, spicy pasta dish that they would make and then sit on their window sills, with the rich smells designed to lure the men in for other services.

Whether or not this is true, it is an amazing dish that is a Fat Paddler signature. I always have the ingredients in the pantry and can throw it together quickly whenever any time last-minute guests arrive. It has never failed to wow them!

Ingredients

- extra virgin olive oil
- 6 anchovies, finely diced
- 2 hot red chillies, finely diced
- 4 cloves of garlic, minced
- 1 tablespoon capers
- 12 kalamata olives
- salt and pepper to taste
- 800 grams tinned tomatoes
- 2 tablespoons brown sugar
- 1 bottle of good red wine (ideally a nice peppery shiraz)
- 500 grams spaghetti
- 200 grams grana padano cheese, finely grated

Method

1 Pour a generous amount of olive oil into a small bowl. Stir in the garlic, anchovies, chillies and capers. Set aside.
2 Crush the olives with the side of a cook's knife and remove the stones. Place in a bowl and set aside.
3 Fill a large pot with hot water and a dash of salt, and place on the stove to boil.
4 Heat a frypan until moderately hot. Add the oil mixture and cook for two to three minutes, stirring occasionally. Don't let the garlic brown! Then stir in the tomatoes and, when they boil, turn the heat down to low. Add brown sugar and stir into the sauce.
5 Add the pasta to the boiling water.
6 Pour a generous glass of red wine. Splash a decent amount into the sauce and stir. Drink the rest.
7 When the pasta is 5 minutes from being cooked, add the olives to the sauce and stir through. Drain the pasta once al dente, and add it to the saucepan, stirring the sauce through. Serve in bowls with a generous sprinkle of grana padano. Buon appetito!

FP's Aussie sausy sanger

I've spent many a Saturday smashing myself on the field of battle known as
the rugby field. It's a crazed sport where you know in your heart that one
of these days a bone will break, something will dislocate, or a tendon will
snap. You don't care, though, because rugby is a gentlemen's game and an
exclusive club. You know that no matter how much you bash or get bashed,
when the final whistle sounds you and your opposite number will shake
hands and have a beer together in the clubrooms. You'll also be ravenously
hungry, and go looking for the barbecue lovingly tended by the lads from
the lower grades. There you'll likely be handed the staple of rugby sideline
food, the sausy sandwich. If you do, don't ask questions, just eat it. You'll
thank me later.

Ingredients

- canola oil (not olive oil)
- 2 lemons, halved
- brown onions, sliced
- green and red peppers, sliced
- jalapeno chillies, sliced
- couple of bottles of cold beer
- sausages
- plenty of butter
- Fresh white bread
- tomato sauce, BBQ sauce, chilli
  sauce, mustard

Method

1 Make sure your barbecue is clean. Rub a little canola oil into the
   hotplate. Then clean the hotplate again using the lemons like scrubbing
   brushes. The acid in the lemons is antiseptic and ensures your barbecue
   is clean and smells nice!
2 Throw on the onions with a dash of oil and push around the hotplate with
   your tongs. Add the sliced peppers and chillies, another dash of oil and
   stir occasionally. After a few minutes, open a bottle of beer, slosh some
   over the mix, then drink the rest. When the mixture looks brownish and
   caramelised, remove and place in a dish.
3 Cook the sausages on the barbecue. The key is to cook them slowly
   over a low heat, turning when required to ensure even cooking. When
   ready, add to the metal dish with the onion mix.
4 Butter a slice of bread liberally and place one or two sausages
   diagonally across it. Add a heap of the onion mix and a generous squirt
   of your favourite sauce (my preference is for chilli sauce). Make sure
   you have some napkins handy and enjoy with another cold beer!

Meat sticks with caramelised balsamic veggies

My two little daughters can be notoriously picky when it comes to dinner, and we struggle to get them to eat everything we cook. Their absolute favourite, however, is lamb cutlets (on the bone), which they lovingly refer to as 'meat sticks'. Smothered with mint jelly and a little gravy on the side, my two princesses munch their way through their meat sticks until their plates are clean. A real success in my book!

Ingredients

Caramelised balsamic veggies
- 1 brown onion, cut into 8 pieces
- 1 Spanish onion, cut into 8 pieces
- 1 red pepper, cut into 8 strips
- 1 green pepper cut into 8 strips
- 1 large fennel, cut into chunks
- 2 carrots, cut into 2-cm pieces
- half a celery, cut into 2-cm pieces
- 1 parsnip, cut into 2-cm pieces
- exta virgin olive oil
- good quality balsamic vinegar

Meat sticks
- 6 lamb cutlets
- extra virgin olive oil
- 3 garlic cloves, crushed
- fresh rosemary

Method

1 Preheat the oven to 200° C. In a large baking pan, add the veggies and pour over a generous dash of olive oil. Pour over a more generous amount of balsamic vinegar and mix through. Place into the oven for approx 40 minutes, turning every 15 minutes.

2 Place the lamb cutlets in a bowl. Add more olive oil, the crushed garlic and ripped handfuls of rosemary leaves. Mix well and let stand until the roast veggies are 10 minutes from being ready.

3 Heat a pan to a moderate–high heat and add the cutlets. After 3–4 minutes, turn and cook the other side. Ideally, remove them while still rare and leave to sit for 5–10 minutes wrapped in foil (unless you like them well done, in which case leave them in the pan a little longer).

4 Spoon out generous heaps of roast veggies onto plates and place a couple of lamb cutlets with each. Crack open a bottle of fine chiraz and enjoy!

Rum drinks for all occasions

My father was never much of a drinker, so you can imagine my surprise when I came home one day back in the nineties to find him sitting on his back porch, holding some sort of tall golden drink stuffed with limes, looking somewhat inebriated. He went on to tell me how in his twenties he had lived in Jamaica, where the rum flowed freely and life was slow and happy. The Barbados rum he'd drunk there, Mount Gay, had never been available in Australia, until earlier that day when he'd discovered it in his local wine shop. It had been over 30 years since he'd had a rum, but that afternoon he bought all the bottles they had and put a serious dent in one of them. Then he sat me down and made me one the way he used to drink it in Jamaica and I was converted at once!

Rum, lime and dry
Dad's Jamaican Special – now popular in the bars of Australia and the world.

Add a handful of ice cubes to a tall glass. Cut two limes in half and squeeze the halves into the glass (add the squished limes into the glass as well). Pour over a generous amount of rum, and fill with cold Dry Ginger Ale.

Black rat
Australia's favourite rum is Bundaberg, known locally as Bundy. They sell pre-packaged cans of Rum and Cola which are nicknamed Black Rats, for the colour of the cans!

Pour a large dash of rum over ice and top up with Coke. It doesn't get much easier or much more Aussie, and they say there's a fight in every glass!

Dark and stormy
Another product by the Bundaberg Rum company, the combination of rum and ginger beer in bottles or cans is the choice of yachties and boaties all over Australia.

Pour a large dash of rum over ice and top up with Ginger Beer. A squeeze of lime or a mint leave garnish is optional.

Taste of summer
When I started playing rugby in Sydney, I found myself in the company of a number of Queenslanders who loved their rum. Our club scrum-doctor, Spanner, would often warm up with what he called a Taste of Summer – Malibu rum and pineapple juice. I found the Malibu a bit sweet, but the idea was a great one. Rum and vitamins all in the one glass!

Pour a large dash of rum over ice and top up with ice-cold pineapple juice. Enjoy!

Acknowledgements

This book would not have been written without the faith shown in my story by Rex Finch and the Finch Publishing team. My editor Samantha Miles showed incredible patience and a willingness to share her knowledge while supporting an insecure writer with too many questions and a deadline phobia. The Finch Marketing and Publicity guru Laura Boon jumped on the Fat Paddler marketing machine with enthusiasm and a deep knowledge of the book game and I thank her for her incredible efforts.

My wife Rebecca is a saint for putting up with my paddling passion. Her ability to deal with my weekly adventures on the water, my nightly forays maintaining my websites, and lately my demand to be locked away in a room to write while leaving her with the kids, has helped me to finish this book. More important was her dedication and care during my last accident – without her love I doubt very much that I would have survived the ordeal.

A special thanks to my two little girls, Grace and Ella, who fill me with joy, laughter and love every single day. You may not realise it now, but every smile, cuddle and kiss you share with me is like a sip from a mountain stream – pure, beautiful and sustaining. Your laughter is my greatest reward.

To my parents Avis and Paul, who have supported me in very different ways over the years. Look, I've actually written a book!

To all the paramedics, doctors and surgeons who together saved my life on more than one occasion, I thank you from the bottom of my heart. A very special thanks to all the nursing staff in our hospitals. The care I received at your hands was amazing, and I am forever indebted to you.

A big thanks to Richard Mullen who first gave me the inspiration to get back into a kayak during his wedding speech, and who helped me get back on my boat so many times on that fateful first paddle.

To all members of Team Fat Paddler (past, present and future), thanks for your friendship and for making our events so much fun. In particular, thanks to Brett Burns, Paul Grummett, Darryl King, Alan Jones, Sacha Ward, Ned Stephenson, Angelo Vassiliades, Nat Bradford, Megan Tassell and Jody Waples.

Thanks to everyone on the North Shore train line who bumped me, yelled at me, squashed me or otherwise distracted me while I wrote this book. That's correct – 80 per cent of this book was written on the train on the way to work!

A huge thanks to Heidi and Matt Cline for looking after a random Aussie in Alaska so well. You do your state and your country proud, I'd travel with you guys again anytime!

Thanks to all the Blue Giants past and present from the great Woollahra Colleagues Rugby Club. Not only are you all a top bunch of blokes, you also managed to introduce me to my wife Rebecca. Thanks also to the Sydney Convicts Rugby Club for accepting an old, fat, lazy, unfit and straight front rower and his wife into your club and making us feel so welcome. My final year of rugby with you all was a blast, as were the odd Saturday nights out at the Shift.

To the touring Colleagues of the 2002 Bali International Rugby Tens, I hope you will forgive me for writing about our experiences. It was by far the hardest part of the book to write, and I hope I have done it justice. A warm thanks also to the people of Bali for their care during the 2002 Bali Bombing. I will never forget your horror at the tragedy that unfolded in Kuta that terrible night, and the support you offered us during your own time of pain. I will never forget any of you.

There are many paddlers, industry people and supporters to thank for sharing their skill, knowledge, friendship and time with me on the water. These include: Shannon O'Brien, Dez Blanchfield, Tim Kennings, Roger Aspinall, Travis Frenay, Chris Mirrow, Sol Kamal, Jen Woods, Adrian Clayton, Conel Gain, Danny Haddad, Jill Ellis, Fiona

Westner-Ramsay, Jim Walton, David AvRutick, Sharon Lovell, Lee Gilbert, Rob Mercer and Domenic Genua.

Thanks to the paddlers who have inspired my drive for adventure: Aussies Justin Jones and James Castrission for paddling across the Tasman, Canadian distance paddler and World Speed record holder Joe O'Blenis, American Greenland rolling champion Helen Wilson, German paddling machine Freya Hoffmeister, extreme sea kayakers the Tsunami Rangers and tide-race lads, the Hurricane Riders.

Lastly, thanks to my grandfather Bill Pollitt, an adventurer who developed his passion for travel from the decks of navy ships during World War II and who never stopped urging me to get out and see the world. Bill passed away peacefully in his sleep before I finished this book and I know he would have been the first to get a copy. I have no doubt he's sipping his ration of Pussers on the deck of the great destroyer in the sky. Rest in Peace, Papa.

You can catch up with Sean Smith through his website
The Fat Paddler at FatPaddler.com or at any of his other
social media sites:

TeamFatPaddler.com

facebook.com/FatPaddler

twitter.com/FatPaddler

twitter.com/TeamFatPaddler

vimeo.com/channels/FatPaddlerTV

youtube.com/FatPaddler

flickr.com/fatpaddler

ZenPaddler.com

GreenlandPaddlers.com